Cyrus Achouri
Modern Systemic Leadership

The author:

 Cyrus Achouri was born in Paris/France. After working for several enterprises (PDI, BMW, Siemens), he now is professor for human resources management at the University of Nuertingen, Germany. His research areas are system theory, leadership and business ethics.

Contact:

Prof. Dr. Cyrus Achouri
University of Nuertingen
Chair in Human Resources Management
Neckarsteige 6-10
72622 Nuertingen/Germany
cyrus.achouri@hfwu.de

# Modern Systemic Leadership

A Holistic Approach for Managers,
Coachs, and HR Professionals

by Cyrus Achouri

PUBLICIS

Bibliographic information published by the Deutsche Nationalbibliothek
The Deutsche Nationalbibliothek lists this publication
in the Deutsche Nationalbibliografie; detailed bibliographic data
are available in the Internet at http://dnb.d-nb.de.

The author and publisher have taken great care with all texts and
illustrations in this book. Nevertheless, errors can never be completely
avoided. The publisher, author and translator accept no liability, regardless of
legal basis. Designations used in this book may be trademarks whose use by
third parties for their own purposes could violate the rights of the owners.

www.publicis.de/books

Translation: Renate Achouri
Contact for authors and editors: gerhard.seitfudem@publicis.de

ISBN 978-3-89578-362-3

Publisher: Publicis Publishing, Erlangen
© 2010 by Publicis KommunikationsAgentur GmbH, GWA, Erlangen

Printed in Germany

# Preface

System Theory has meanwhile established itself within many scientific disciplines and has shown productive results. However, a systematic-scientific adaptation for the management theory, especially for personnel management, has not taken place up to now – at least, I do not know of any. I therefore would like to make a contribution to encourage the discussion on how we can take advantage of some systemic axioms in the field of personnel management.

In order to understand what contribution Systemic Leadership in management can offer, we will begin by presenting general principles of personnel management and development. After an introduction to essential management tools like feedback, coaching, performance management and human resources controlling (Chapters 2 and 3), fundamental management methods will follow, including ethical aspects (Chapters 4 and 5). In Chapter 6, we will deal with international personnel management aspects in a globalized world as well as some essential paradigms of intercultural leadership. In Chapter 7, we present different systemic models as part of disciplines like biology, evolution theory, physics, cognitive sciences, philosophy, pedagogics, sociology and management. Finally, in Chapter 8, I attempt to bring in all these ideas in one theory of Systemic Leadership.

The contents of this book resulted from the lectures held in the summer term 2008 and the winter term 2008/2009 at the University of Nuertingen. I am grateful for the numerous suggestions by my students whom I want to thank cordially. Also do I want to thank Dr. Gerhard Seitfudem, Business Director at Publicis for making this book happen and a very big Thank You to Renate Achouri for the translation.

This book is intended equally for Students to accompany the lectures in Business Administration with focus on Personnel Management, and for interested Executives and Personnel Managers who, in their enterprises, want to put into practice an extended catalogue of management tools.

My wish to all of you is that reading may bring you fun and benefit.

*Nuertingen, January 2010*
*Cyrus Achouri*

# Contents

*"But anguish crept upon me,*
*Whenas I pondered in my little cell:*
*Ah me! how have I come into this evil road.*
*Into the power of Craving have I strayed!*
*Brief is the span of life yet left to me;*
*Old age, disease, hang imminent to crush.*
*Now ere this body perish and dissolve,*
*Swift let me be; no time have I for sloth.*
*And contemplating, as they really are,*
*The Aggregates of Life that come and go,*
*I rose and stood with mind emancipate!"*
Psalms of the Early Buddhists

# Chapter 1

# Introduction

*"If you want to build a ship, don't drum up the men to
gather wood, divide the work and give orders. Instead teach
them to yearn for the vast and endless sea."*

Antoine de Saint-Exupéry

Any company nowadays knows that performance and motivation of
their employees are being influenced mostly by its quality of leadership
(more than 70%[1]). Excellent leadership today by no means is only an
ideal but a condition sine qua non of successful entrepreneurship.
There are several reasons for that.

One of them is that because of a lack of qualified manpower there is
not only a need to win over the best talents but also to retain them.
This achievement is expected from the direct executive personnel. In
many cases where companies take the record of resignation interviews,
one can observe a direct correlation between bad leadership and unwel-
come fluctuation of employees.

Also, changing demands by employees concerning the degree of independence in their work, the combination of career and profession in
different working and time models, the so-called work-life balance, are
important points especially for highly qualified employees and all the
more so for the considerable female part among them. Any excuse by
executives as to increased coordination cost for part-time workers or
lacking efficiency is not accepted any more as a reason to refuse flexible
working models. A great number of studies prove that part-time
employees deal even more efficiently with their working hours. They
are simply forced to do so.

While technical possibilities of rationalization can be perfected more
and more asymptotically, we are rather at the beginning when it comes
to the activation of the resource "employee motivation". Employee

---

[1]  IES Report 355, From People to Profits, 1999

motivation, however, is essential for willingness to perform as well as for efficiency and it is therefore imperative to specifically use this first domino and to understand that excellent leadership is the central leverage for the success of an enterprise.

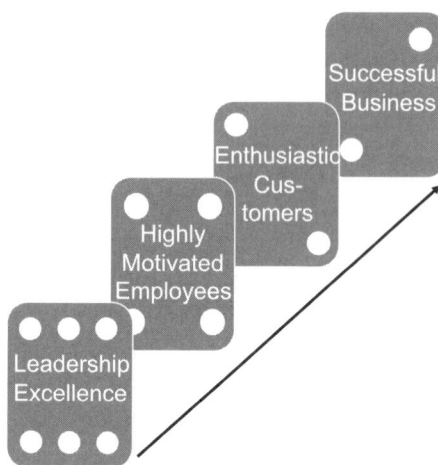

**Figure 1**
"Leadership Domino"

In this book you will not find an introduction into the entire subject of Human Resources Management. However, we will present main subjects of particular importance for Human Resources Management and subsequently deduce "Systemic Leadership" as systemic approach to HR-Management. The method will not be historical, but systematic.

In Chapter 2 we will start by looking into performance management systems for performance evaluation. We present basic techniques like feedback and communication analysis, both of which should be basic knowledge of any executive. We will then talk about the staff dialogue and the upward feedback which are complementary to each other. Finally, relevant HR-performance indicators will be discussed allowing to define performance objectives and to measure their achievement, especially by using the balanced score card as controlling instrument.

Chapter 3 offers an introduction to executive coaching. Despite their relevance for management performance, no consistently formulated quality standards for the training and use of coaches are yet available. We will define quality criteria for the selection of coaches as well as criteria for successful controlling and evaluation. This Chapter will close with an introduction of selected consulting approaches that are applied in executive coaching.

Chapter 4 attempts to answer the question which value system may be able to support executives when operating in delicate personnel situations, and Chapter 5 presents some theories of leadership. Following an introduction to employee motivation, images of man as basic paradigms are presented that have always been an underlying part of the style and understanding of leadership. We will then introduce selected management styles and finally present the so-called management techniques, i.e. the craft skills to put them into practice.

Chapter 6 deals with HR- management on a globalized level and presents strategies of internationalization as well as different models to describe intercultural aspects. This closes the introduction to principal leadership theorems.

Chapter 7 offers an excursion to different scientific disciplines which allow to present system theory in its principal statements. We examine the statements of evolutionary biology, physics, chaos research, cognitive sciences or philosophy, pedagogics and management theory in order to find out the common aspects.

These common aspects we will use as a basis in Chapter 8 in order to apply the systemic statements and results to personnel management and set up a draft of Systemic Leadership.

# Chapter 2

# Performance Management Systems

*"My main job was developing talent. I was a gardener*
*providing water and other nourishment to our top 750 people.*
*Of course, I had to pull out some weeds, too."*

Jack Welch (*19.11.1935),
former CEO of General Electric (1981-2001)

Performance management means the process of performance measurement, performance steering and performance control of individual employees, teams and executives. The objective of this process is a continued improvement of individual performance ending up in an improved performance of the whole enterprise. Extending its attention from accountancy with its main interest on the past, performance management also focuses on non-financial performance indicators. This comprehensive planning and steering process is additionally brought into line with future challenges.

In order to meet this comprehensive objective, many companies use the balanced score card in order to measure financial results, process efficiency as well as employee and customer satisfaction. Below, we will present important performance management instruments, the staff dialogue und its complementary tool, the upward feedback.

The basis of all these instruments, however, is communication. Structured and successful communication is a management tool by itself already, and any applied methods of performance management depend on the quality of communication involved. When talking of communication used for reporting back information on behaviour and performance, the term "feedback" has gained acceptance following the scientific concept of back coupling.

Before looking into the methods themselves, we should therefore pay attention to the basics of successful communication. Especially feedback does play an important role here as it is a communication instrument that reports back information on behaviour and performance.

## 2.1 Feedback

### 2.1.1 The meaning of "feedback"

Although feedback has probably become the best-known management instrument at all and employees as well as executives do well know the rules of feedback by theory and training, when put into practice, however, there is either a lack of comprehension of the subject or there is not sufficient conviction to use this knowledge successfully. In any case, in the average business practice, an increase in positive communicational culture cannot be observed.

At the same time it is a fact that giving feedback and taking feedback are the most important tools in personnel management and development. Supposing we were forced to refrain from any Human Resources Management Tools at all, we still could not do without a productive and orderly communication. There is an enormous gap between the relevance which feedback should have and which it does actually enjoy in the perception of executives.

The best way to work on a productive feedback culture certainly is to combine the theoretical input with directly following practice. Only training creates the understanding for the existing (and often unconscious) communication patterns and only training will break up communication and behaviour patterns that have been existing for a long time. A purely cognitive and conscious approach will mostly not be sufficient. Only role playing in training will show how far the theoretical contents have really been understood and internalized. Therefore, at the beginning, self assessment and result after training may be a long way away from each other.

Feedback is an especially interesting tool. It is not only relevant resp. has not been particularly designed for executives or employees. It is, on the contrary, a communication pattern that can be applied to all fields of human communication. This is the reason why most feedback trainings request that the theory should be applied and trained as often as possible in the private field and in this way be made an individual and personal communication pattern.

Practice shows that it takes a certain time until one is able to formulate for instance the three-step feedback rules in such a way that they do not seem learned by heart or put on stage. Especially when dealing with peer colleagues in business or with people in the private field it can turn out to be a considerable challenge to formulate feedback professionally without losing one's own authenticity and naturalness.

In Human Resources Management, the situation is different. Here, values like authenticity and naturalness are of course also desirable for an executive who expects to be accepted by the employees. However, what we have to bear in mind here additionally is an existing appraisal situation with all possible consequences. Therefore, in the communication between executive and employees, the objective has to be on the one hand clearness and precision of the statements, and on the other hand an inoffensive tone. If these aspects of communication are fulfilled by the executive, the employee will regard the conversation as professional even if the rules of feedback are not internalized entirely and are formulated perhaps clumsily or with difficulty.

Contrary to the unprofessional, chatty tone of an executive with ambiguous authenticity, the conscious compliance to formal feedback rules expresses also verbally that the appraisal process is respected and that the executive is explicitly trying to cope with the task of evaluation. Let us now talk about the contents of this communication.

## 2.1.2 Communication Analysis

Feedback as an instrument as well as specifically recommended feedback rules are a result of the work of social psychologists and group dynamic experts like for instance Kurt Lewin. Feedback means reporting back to an individual information about his behaviour and how this behaviour is perceived, understood and experienced by others. Such feedback is permanently happening when we are in contact with others, consciously or unconsciously, spontaneously or upon request, verbally or by non-verbal communication, i. e. body language. In order to make these processes conscious, to train them and to improve self and counterpart perception, feedback has been used for a long time in group-dynamic training. The task is to verify one's self perception and to adjust it with the perceptions from others. Such an adjustment is being described for instance with the "Johari Window".

### Johari Window

The Johari Window is a window of conscious as well as unconscious personality and behaviour characteristics between an individual and others, resp. another group. It was developed 1955 by the American Social Psychologists Joseph Luft and Harry Ingham[1] and "Johari" is a combination of both their first names. By means of the Johari Window we can illustrate the so-called blind spot in the self perception of an individual.

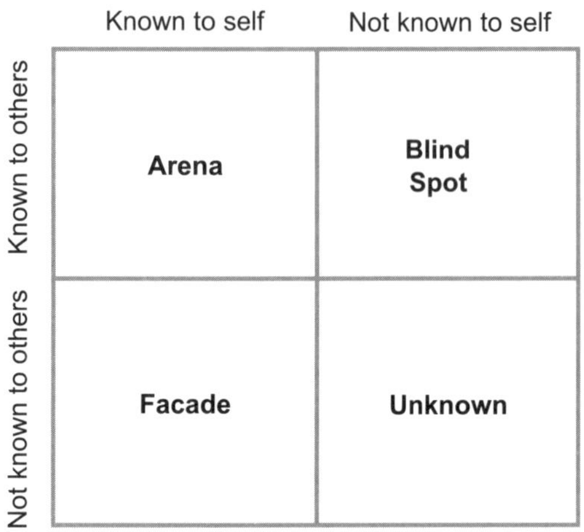

|  | Known to self | Not known to self |
|---|---|---|
| **Known to others** | Arena | **Blind Spot** |
| **Not known to others** | **Facade** | **Unknown** |

**Figure 2** Johari Window

The "Arena" as the Public Person includes everything that an individual reveals about himself, i. e. everything that is conscious to himself and others. It is the part that is being made visible to the outside. This part, in comparison to the other parts, is mostly rather small. However, essential for the quality of relationships are the non-public parts.

"Facade" is everything that is known by the individual but that he does not make accessible to others or that he actively hides from them, also known as "Secret".

By "Blind Spot", we understand information which is not known by the individual himself but which, however, others do know.

Finally, the "Unknown" is defined by information that is not known by the individual nor others. Sigmund Freud called it the unconscious.

---

[1] Luft, J. & Ingham, H. 1955

One essential learning objective in group dynamic training is to expand and make more transparent the common room for manoeuvre. When applying this to the Johari Window, the left upper field becomes bigger and bigger, while the other three fields become smaller and smaller.

By informing the individual in question directly about blind spots, he will gain knowledge about himself and will be able to perceive more consciously his private and public room for manoeuvre and so take better advantage of it. The question "What" is being efficiently supported by the question "How" contained in the feedback rules.

Another well-known illustration of conscious and unconscious parts in the communication is the "Iceberg Model", which goes back to the Psychoanalyst Sigmund Freud.

### Iceberg Model

According thereto, only a relatively small part of the communication takes place on the surface of the ocean – the visible iceberg. The much bigger part of non-verbal, emotional and unconscious communication lies within the ocean, hidden from direct perception.

**Figure 3** Iceberg Model

This fact was also taken into account by Ruth Cohn (*1912)[1], Psycho-analyst and Founder of the Concept of Theme Centered Interaction (TCI), when formulating: "Disturbances have Priority".

According to her, it is essential, especially when working with groups, to make existing (emotional) disturbances that become felt in communication a subject of discussion, to bring them on the upper side of the iceberg and in that way to make possible an objective and conscious clarification. If we are not ready to allow priority to these disturbances, they will anyway take hold of the situation, with or without our consent.

The result will probably be that the group process and an objective clarification of tasks and problems is thrown back. TCI enumerates four essential factors in the group process, the individual concern (I), the needs of the group (We), the task (It) and the environment (Globe).

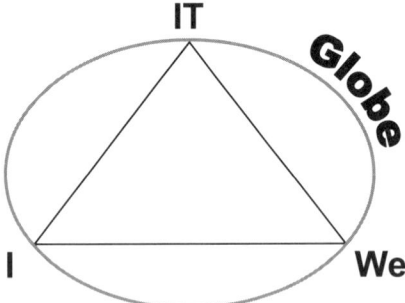

**Figure 4** TCI Triangle

Also, the famous mime artist and Professor emeritus of the Vienna Conservatory, Samy Molcho (*1916 in Tel Aviv)[2], showed in his analysis of our body language impressively that there is a huge part of non-verbal and unconscious elements in our communication.

---

[1] Cohn, 1975
[2] Molcho, 2001

## The Four Sides Model (Communication Square)

Another model for communication analysis is the Four Sides Model by Schulz von Thun[1]. Any information/message is sent by the sender (=encoded), then transmitted and finally picked up by the addressee (decoded). In the process of encoding and decoding serious translating errors may arise.

The reasons may be manifold, for instance technical disturbances (noise in the telephone), language difficulties (foreign language). Any sender talks in four tongues, any addressee hears with four ears. The danger exists that sender and addressee put a different weight to the four sides of a message or interpret it differently altogether.

The four sides of a message are the levels of 1) matter, 2) relationship, 3) self-revealing, and 4) appeal. For instance, one may hear a distinct appeal in the message of the partner although he only wanted to communicate something about his actual feelings or to describe an objective fact. Example: wife and husband sit at the dinner table. Husband: "There is something green in the soup." Answer from the wife: "If you don't like it, why don't you cook yourself."

The Communication Square assumes that any statement can be interpreted towards four different sides – by the sender of the statement as well as by the addressee.

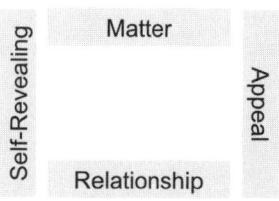

**Figure 5**
Communication Square[2]

On the matter side (top), the speaking person informs on the objective content, i. e. data and facts. The self-revealing (left) contains what the speaking person makes known about himself by sending his message. On the relationship side (bottom) is expressed what kind of relation-

---

[1] Schulz von Thun, 1981

[2] According to Friedemann Schulz von Thun, www.schulz-von-thun.de

ship the sender has to the addressee and what he thinks of him. The appeal side (right) shows what the sender would like to arrive at with the addressee.

Johari window, iceberg model and communication square are examples for the analysis of communication. They do not yet offer an action pattern or a recommendation as to how communication could or should take place, but they describe what aspects are contained in human communication and how they work.

We now come to the specific recommendations for communication as, for instance, they are made in the feedback rules.

### Rules of Feedback

As a matter of principle, any feedback should be given by the feedback sender only in those cases where the feedback taker wishes to do so. This makes certainly sense within the circle of peer working colleagues. In the case of executives it is only partially applicable for two reasons: on the one hand, staff dialogue that contains feedback on the performance of the employee has its fixed place in the performance management process and is firmly prescribed anyway. On the other hand there is an obligation by the executive to give feedback to his employees without being invited in all cases of behaviour assessment that will, later on, be part of the performance evaluation.

Any executive, therefore, has the obligation, depending on the situation, to actively address his employees, and not only offer feedback but actually transmit it. Apart from that, the feedback process as it takes place in the communication from executive to employee will not differ from any other feedback process.

In the feedback process, the addressee has the possibility to learn what effect he has on others. That gives him a chance to think about if he wants to keep the situation as it is or to possibly change his behaviour. In human relations many things are kept secret or communication takes place under cover, as we have seen in the iceberg model or the Yohari window. An open feedback has the effect that what was hidden will be consciously taken notice of. Desires and needs, joy and recognition can be exchanged and fears and injuries discussed. This will make grow understanding, reliability and finally trust.

Especially in groups, emotions will often be swept aside and may then develop negative effects. Conflicts also arise in the case of contradictory objectives. In an open feedback, emotions can be disclosed and motives and needs explained. This may lead to clarity which, in its turn, may result in a better cooperation. In the following, we present the three-step Feedback "Burger" Rules.

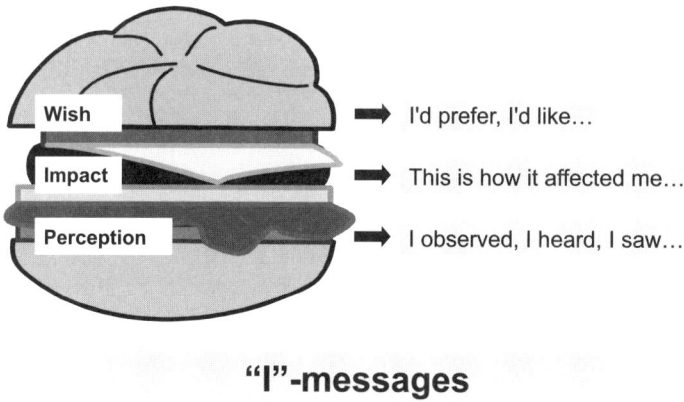

## "I"-messages

**Figure 6** Feedback Burger Rules

According to these rules, feedback is formulated by 1) perception, 2) impact, 3) wish. Starting point always is a perceived and observed behaviour. Perceived behaviour here is understood on a sensuous level, i. e. in the business context mainly visually and aural.

In the second step, the feedback sender describes the impact which is released by the perceived behaviour. This effect necessarily is subjective and will therefore most probably have very different implications, depending on the individual involved. Consequently, it makes sense to formulate this message in the first person, thereby avoiding sharpness and putting the message into a subjective perspective.

In the last step, a wish can be formulated in which the feedback sender – again in the first-person approach – wishes for the modification in behaviour of the feedback addressee.

At this point, one may consider if it makes sense to really formulate a wish, because any wish, even when formulated in the first person, is a request to the addressee to change. The solution could be to formulate the third step as "proposal" or "alternative" and to formulate accordingly. Instead of: "I would wish for this or that change on your part", one could say: "If you acted in this or that way, it would not lead to this (negative) reaction on my side, but that reaction (positive)".

This procedure is so effective because it is transmitted in a non-offensive way. No statements on the personality are made that could be injuring ("You are a....human being!"). On the contrary, on a level of objective reality, a sensuously observable behaviour is addressed which leads to a subjective personal request. This offers two special advantages:

On the one hand, pure perception relates to something that the feedback taker has (hopefully) also realized, although, of course, it cannot be excluded that this perception was not conscious to the feedback taker or is being simply denied by him or her. Once, however, the basis for a common perception has been created, it is easier to enter into discussion on how this behaviour was meant and what effect it has had.

On the other hand, describing the specific behaviour offers to the feedback taker the possibility of a productive reaction and a possible change. If for instance an executive says to his employee "You are unreliable", the effect on the employee will be an offensive one. Making the same statement according to feedback rules it may, as an example, be expressed as follows: "You regularly are late for our meetings by five to ten minutes. This disturbs the order of events and it has the effect on me as if you did not take seriously my appointments. My wish would be that from now on you arrived punctually to our meetings".

This creates a non-offensive environment for communication and the employee finds out very exactly how he can change his behaviour in order to release a different reaction by his executive.

Business practice shows that this kind of communication is also more adequate to the feedback taker who, very often, is not aware of the own behaviour and even more so of its effect on others. Mostly, the own behaviour is not at all meant as a provocation – it is just not reflected upon. An offensive statement concerning the whole person as shown above could possibly be completely wrong and be a subject of offence in itself. Maybe it helps to keep in mind a thought by the philosopher Sokrates, according to which man does not act consciously with bad intention but because of missing insight. Feedback helps to create insight.

## Limits of Feedback

This statement of Heraklit may also be said about feedback as communication tool. The use of feedback and its justification cannot be applied without limits. To set limits is necessary in order to prevent that feedback as a tool becomes a weapon of communication.

It was already mentioned before that feedback processes on peer levels (for example with colleagues or in private life) have to be distinguished from their application as management instrument. As we saw already, an executive should not wait for the employee to ask for feedback.

It would be inappropriate to thank the feedback sender for his information as the transmitted content is not only destined to be used by the feedback taker for his personal development but is meant as basis for his specific performance appraisal.

One further important point is the relevance that a given feedback has for the appliance by the feedback taker. It is up to the feedback taker alone if he wants to accept the feedback. This is as well relevant for the situation executive vs. employee, although here the consequences to be expected are different from those applicable when dealing with colleagues.

Relevant for the executive is the feedback instrument only in the limits which the content of the feedback has with regard to the job. Any statements that do not directly concern the working field and are not intended to improve working cooperation, are not part of the executive's area of responsibility.

For example, it is not admissible for an executive to address feedback extended to the person as a whole, resp. his general way of life, his ethical attitude, etc. Advice can be very hurting, especially when given by a person with authority to the feedback taker or within a hierarchy of power, as this is the case between executive and employee. From the view of the employee, the limit of feedback runs along the point where he rejects the adaptation of the feedback to his own behaviour.

With regard to the executive as a person, the employee also has to make a decision as to the acceptability of wishes for modification of behaviour. The question that has to be answered by the employee is in how far he is willing and able to comply with the wishes for modification in behaviour adapting to a specific company culture as requested by his executive who, in his turn, represents the enterprise. This decision will regularly have to be an individual one for each case.

For the executive as well as for the employee it is important to understand that the feedback tool is not meant to be an instrument to formulate unlimited wishes to a particular individual which the feedback taker then has to comply with. In reality we are approached with numerous wishes every day which we can not possibly meet. The consequence of adapting to all these wishes would in the extreme case mean to destroy one's own will.

Particularly executives have to learn, often painfully, that they cannot please all their employees all of the time, even if they wanted to. The power of self-assertion, however, is a quality that an executive has to have or has to learn. It implies a critical examination of one's own behaviour, especially with the help of feedback from others, but it also implies the ability to reject demands which one cannot or does not want to meet.

> *"I am myself and you are yourself. I am not*
> *in this world to be as you wish me to be and you are not*
> *in this world to be as I wish you to be."*
> *Fritz Perls[1]*

After having been introduced to the basics of successful communication, we now want to see different processes of performance management where these communication structures are used.

## 2.2 Staff Dialogue

The staff dialogue is an instrument where executive and employee discuss normally once a year (with additional reviews during the year) topics like agreement on the objectives, assessment of past performance, personal and professional training, general development possibilities in the enterprise, etc.

Often the conversation is based on personnel forms, guides, check lists or other forms that serve as a structure for leading the conversation by

---

[1] Fritz Perls (1893-1970), Psychotherapist and Co-Founder of the "Gestalt-Therapy"

the executive, but also help to maintain comparability between the whole group of employees evaluated.

Although content and elements are optional and should be adapted to special business needs, there is a comparable basic structure to be recommended to a staff dialogue.

It goes without saying that the Staff Dialogue like any other feedback instrument that is being used by an enterprise (e. g. Upward Feedback, Staff Survey, 360° Feedback, Assessment Center etc.) has to be coordinated with the work council and possibly to be put down in company agreements.

A staff dialogue can take place on different occasions, for instance at the end of probation time, at the end of a set time limit, at termination of an employment contract by annulment or notice, for performance and potential assessments, training, change of area of responsibility, return after disablement or illness, career development, analysis of conflict, etc. Starting point is the job description which is the basis of the job profile.

After having discussed the tasks assigned, normally a review of the past year follows. A statement is being made as to the degree of achievement of the different tasks and the underlying reason.

Then the objectives for the following year (or in the case of a new function, perhaps for the next six months) are agreed upon and possibly an appointment is fixed for a review in a few months' time in order to verify if the employee is on the right path to meet his objectives and to correct this path, if necessary.

Another subject of discussion should be the medium-term and long-term career planning, and, if applicable, measurements for training that could support this development. As to the contents of staff dialogues, perspectives of the balanced score card, for example, could be adopted (see Chapter 2.5.1).

The conversation should take place in a quiet atmosphere without time pressure and without disturbance. For a staff dialogue that is scheduled once a year, one hour should certainly be reserved.

Mutual esteem should be expressed, not only at the beginning and at the end, but it should indeed be the basis for the whole meeting. It helps to stick to the feedback rules as they objectivise communication and offer a basis for proceeding.

**Figure 7** Staff Dialogue Process

After the dialogue meeting between executive and employee, the executive should present his employee assessment as well as the proposed further steps in the career planning to a peer group of executives.

By this procedure, one avoids major "blind spots" in the executive's employee assessment as it does give a frame for a comparative evaluation. Statements on performance have to be calibrated by being adjusted with the evaluations of the other representatives of the executive committee.

The calibration after which performance is being qualified as average, above average or below average does not only depend on comparisons with other employees but also on the strategic goals of the enterprise, open jobs, number of potentials, different qualifications at disposal, etc.

A simple and final assessment of the employee solely by his executive obviously could not only be unfair but it could also be in conflict with the interests of the enterprise.

Thus, during the performance management process, the staff dialogue between executive and employee is followed by the presentation and evaluation of its results within a superior executive committee which, in its turn, is followed again by a feedback from the direct executive to his employee transmitting to him his confirmed evaluation results.

## 2.3 Upward Feedback

*"For those with whom I work it is imperative that they
also criticize myself. If they don't do that they are of no use
to me and to the house of Siemens."*

C. F. von Siemens

While the staff dialogue concerns the performance assessment of the
employee, the upward feedback aims at the assessment of executives by
their employees.

Staff Dialogue and Upward Feedback are complementary and finally
form the performance management process as a whole.

Any company interested in a continuous improvement of Human Resources Performance Management and in creating an open company
culture is well advised to use the chances of employee feedback.

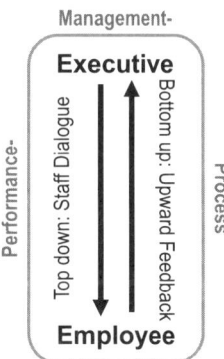

**Figure 8**
Performance Management Process

The upward feedback deals with the relationship between superior and
employee by having the executive evaluated by his employees. It aims
especially at the evaluation of the leadership performance of the superior.

Although there is empirical proof that anonymously evaluating employees will rate their superiors less well than those that make their
statements openly,[1] there are good reasons to practice semi-anonymous

---

[1] Voltz, 1998, 61

personal conversations. In that way an upward feedback carried out within a workshop may be used at the same time as team development measure.

At the same time, using such an instrument presents an intervention in the sense of the organizational development of an enterprise and is appropriate to help along the establishment of a cooperative leadership culture as well as a company culture based on trust and open dialogue, provided this is explicit part of the company strategy.

The idea of upward feedback as a performance management instrument is relatively recent as it breaks up the traditional role behaviour (top down procedure) and limits executives in their power privilege. A certain dependency from the employees may establish itself as these are now in a position to issue a report to their executives.

In the course of the establishment of participative and teamspirit-oriented leadership styles, however, the role itself of the executive has changed. Today, an executive is much more a consultant and team player for whom values like partnership-based and team-oriented behaviour should have priority.

The direct reason for an upward feedback may be bad work climate, criticism on the part of the employees toward their executives, or an intended comparison between target vs. actual values contained in the existing management guidelines of the enterprise.

Notwithstanding this deficit strategy for problem solving, many enterprises now establish upward feedback assessments without special reason as integral part of their performance management process and repeat it at regular intervals as a complementary measure to employee assessment.

It is a good idea to carefully keep separate in time schedule employee and superior assessments within the performance management process. An upward feedback taking place directly before an employee assessment is not recommendable because employees may not feel free to make certain statements, especially critical ones, fearing that this could have an effect to their disadvantage in their own appraisal.

Also, attention should be paid to the fact that in case the upward feedback is being carried out during a workshop, the number of assessing employees is big enough to allow for a relatively anonymous group feedback without exposing any particular employee unduly. Experience shows that a minimum of six or seven employees should be part of the assessing group.

To the executive, the feedback provides information in how far self-image and outside image differ from each other, i. e. how the own behaviour is perceived by employees and how it differs from one's own evaluation.

In this field, often a big discrepancy will appear. Therefore it is recommendable to work with feedback rules in order to create as much as possible a matter-of-fact atmosphere without hostility. For this reason, feedback rules are integral part of any upward feedback procedure that is carried out non-electronic, within the frame of a personal exchange.

The instrument of upward feedback gives a chance to the employees to have influence and to take over responsibility with regards to shaping the relationship with their executive. In how far this influence remains only an emotional one or really contributes to a change in the quality of leadership and company culture, not only depends on the understanding and acceptance of criticism by the executive, but also on the quality of the concept of the performance management process established by the enterprise.

We can observe a wide range in the readiness of companies to put these methods into practice – from the establishment of purely formal executive assessments up to the actual linking of parts of the executive compensation to the results of the assessment. As middle course, practice shows that often a certain transparency concerning the assessment results, for example in the intranet of a company, can have a considerable effect.

What is to be aimed at with the upward feedback finally is the improvement of the relationship between executives and employees, an increase in motivation and performance and the establishment of an open dialogue culture. Mutual respect and a company culture that is trusting and free from fear should be the objective.

In the focus of the upward feedback should not be the apportioning of blame but a common effort to improve cooperation to the profit of the enterprise as a whole.

A positive evaluation may have the effect that the executive gets a positive attitude to participative leadership and cooperation, and he may derive concrete ideas for his own personnel development. An executive may react with increased interest in his own quality of leadership or on the contrary, in the case of a negative assessment, with repulse and resistance.

Often the feedback causes a feeling of uncertainty on the part of the executive concerning the own management behaviour, and this especially on the part of young executives who do not have any experience yet with assessments concerning their management role.

For employees, the upward feedback usually is an instrument to which they react with an increase in motivation and in self-esteem as well as with improved performance within the team. However, another reaction may as well be fear of sanctions, unrealistic expectations as to concrete changes, a feeling that too much is expected or overestimation of one's own influence on changing processes.

Resignation may turn up, especially in cases where employees put expectations into the instrument that then cannot be met for different reasons. Such reasons may be a stubborn executive, bad moderation of a feedback workshop or simply excessive expectations that focus for instance on a revolutionary change of the whole working environment and therefore are unrealistic. However, it remains important that the results of the assessment have concrete consequences and start evident changes.

The effects of the upward feedback as a performance management instrument can be manifold for the enterprise as a whole. It is to be expected that the introduction of this instrument represents a major intervention in the organizational development. It will have effects on the communication culture, the management guidelines as well as the leadership style as a whole.

The introduction of the upward feedback as performance management system without the active promotion of a participative, team-oriented leadership culture is doomed to failure right from the beginning. The assessment represents an early warning system for loss of motivation and performance orientation on the part of the employees. However, an enterprise has to be careful not to stigmatize executives after bad evaluations, but on the contrary to use the feedback offer as an instrument for a continuous personnel development procedure.

Another controversial point is the qualification of the employees assessing their superiors. There certainly can and will occur evaluation mistakes as well as subjective perception and evaluation errors (Halo-, Primacy-, Recency-Effect etc.). Assuming that it is correct that an executive will always be only as good as his employees see him and considering that most of the time executives cannot choose their employees as employees cannot choose their executives, it does not seem unreasonable that executives should take up the challenge of an upward feedback by their group of employees and that employee qualification should not matter.

## 2.3.1 Moderated Workshop

Hereunder, we would like to present an example for the course of an upward feedback in the form of a moderated dialogue-supported workshop with card questioning. Using a workshop or a moderated dialogue between executive and employees offers many advantages in comparison to methods supported by questionnaires or electronics.

There are many details that disappear within a purely anonymous method by questionnaire, but that come to the surface in a moderated workshop and may make the feedback clearer and more human. Pressure, of course, for employees as well as for the executive is higher in a personal exchange, however by the face-to-face feedback the exchange becomes at the same time more direct and brings to light latent and hidden statements and assumptions.

All participants have to be informed in detail in advance, preferably by the person that will moderate the process. In large companies, for this task should be asked especially trained employees from the Human Resources Department whose function allows neutrality in moderation.

A few weeks before the planned date of the upward feedback, the moderator will have a preliminary meeting with the executive in order to clarify details as to organization and content. This may include the introduction of the executive to the instrument itself, the delegation of the administrative responsibility like booking of the room, catering, etc. as well as for example details on difficult employees, discontentment to be expected, latest developments within the department, etc.

Although normally it is up to the executive to freely choose the moderator, constellations should be avoided which make the moderator seem prejudiced in any way. Also no moderator should be chosen who may have been involved in any unfavourable past incident. On the date of the workshop, one resp. several suitable rooms need to be prepared. One larger room offering enough space for plenum work by the employees should be available, as well as two to three smaller rooms for group work. For time reasons and clarity's sake a moderator should not form more than four groups. As each group makes its presentation one after the other, four groups are the maximum of what can be dealt with as regards duration and focused, active participation.

A suitable setting in the plenum could be, like in other workshop variations, the open circle of chairs which will contribute, after having removed all tables, to reduce distance between the participants. It is useful to have the executive sit on the one side of the circle and all employees on the other side. Moderation tools will be the usual mixture of laptop and beamer, overhead projector as well as flipchart and pin wall.

General information, for example, can be transmitted as animation by laptop or as step-by-step information on the flipchart. As actual medium for the feedback moderation, a pin wall is very suitable as it allows to cluster, i. e. to arrange cards according to subjects, as well as a rapid rearrangement or change of the visualization. A pin wall furthermore calls for cards to be pinned on.

The workshop meeting should begin with the executive welcoming his own employees and introduce the moderator. This demonstrates that the event is being carried out by the executive and wanted by him. Welcome phase and goodbye phase are presented by the executive. After the introduction, the executive passes on the direction of the meeting to the moderator. This latter will point out his special role as moderator, in case his normal function in the enterprise is a different one.

Then the time has come to introduce the instrument of upward feedback to the employees. In those cases in which the evaluation has a regular and binding place within the performance management process of the enterprise, it will be sufficient to talk about the main points like order of event, feedback culture in the workshop, role of the instrument within the personnel resp. organizational development in the enterprise, etc.

Now, the employees are asked, within groups, to gather information concerning the management performance and to discuss it, while the executive for himself tries to set up criteria for successful and less successful management behaviour derived from the daily professional routine.

Unless there are special reasons against it, the groups between the employees should be formed by chance, by means of coloured cards or by simple counting up. The random selection of the group composition serves a more neutral working climate and the team development. Employees may come together who, under normal circumstances, do not have any direct contact in their work.

It makes sense to divide the quality of the management performance into two criteria, 1) successfull leadership, and 2) development potential. The distributed cards to employees and executive should be distinguished by colour and form. For example, green cards may stand for successful leadership and white or yellow cards for development potential. A quantitative limitation in cards up to a maximum of three cards per criterion and per group will ensure that the time frame can be kept.

The criteria should be exactly formulated and precisely determined – a necessity that applies to any direction of group work. For instance, for the employees, it could be questions like "What kind of behaviour should be kept on by my executive?", "What works well already in our department?", resp. "What kind of behaviour should be changed by my executive?" As regards the executive, he could find an answer to the questions "Where are my strengths in leadership?", resp. "Where is room for improvement in my leadership performance?"

Differently from anonymous (electronic or not) questionnaire methods, the discussion in small groups will enable the employees to put into perspective their own perceptions and evaluations and to arrive at a more objective judgment on the management performance of their executive. As additional help for the employees, the company performance guidelines should be put at their disposal as criteria according to which the performance of the executive should be evaluated. In that context it becomes clear exactly what standard of demands the executive should meet.

After the self evaluation of the executive as well as the group works are finished, the moderator may explain the feedback rules as fundamentals of communication based on esteem. They will be needed and should be agreed upon for the following feedback dialogue. At this stage, once again the confidentiality of the workshop should be pointed out and the participants should be reminded that the feedback information given in the workshop should not leave the room.

Thus the basis of communication having been clarified, the moderator asks the executive to start with his self evaluation. Before the meeting, the moderator will have agreed upon with the executive with what criteria, the strengths or the development potential, the latter wants to start. In case the executive does not have any special preference, it is recommendable to start with the development potential so that the strengths of the executive are placed at the end of the workshop and thus make possible a positive conclusion.

The executive having explained his cards and having pinned them on the pin wall, the small groups of employees start to introduce those of their cards that refer directly to the self evaluation of the executive. The moderator will – not without asking the consent of the author before – arrange them to sensible clusters on the pin wall so that in the progress of the meeting, main areas of subjects and priorities will be discovered.

At this feedback stage which constitutes the essence of the upward feedback process, the moderator will, if necessary, repeatedly remind the participants of the agreement to stick to a way of communication based on esteem and according to feedback rules. Experience shows that the moderator will also have to remind the executive that feedback should not be commented on and that there should be no justification by the executive concerning the statements made. Allowed are, of course, questions as to comprehension.

After all the feedback information to development potential has been given, the moderator will terminate this stage of feedback. This will prevent that especially critical or negative employees repeatedly keep on talking in the further course of the meeting. This point of termination can be stressed if the moderator makes a statement that this is now the last possibility to make a comment to the development potential and that he asks explicitly for confirmation by the employees that from now on the subject will change to the strengths.

The feedback as to the positive management behaviour is treated in the same way as described above with the development potential, and all cards are arranged to clusters. With this, the essential feedback dialogue is finished.

While the employees have a break, the executive and the moderator will use this time to prepare a target agreement. As is the case with any evaluation, the essential result must be that measures to be taken are deducted. Possibly not all subjects gathered under the topic "development potential" can be taken up. Depending upon the subjects, a natural limit on the number to be taken up is recommended. Normally, a maximum of three main areas should not be exceeded and priorities within them established. They will be made part of the target agreement.

It is part of the executive's role to make a choice between the subjects. The moderator cannot do this for him and even more so, any kind of influence or manipulation by the moderator has to be avoided. The role of the moderator when preparing the target agreement is solely to serve the executive as coach, thus enabling him to choose three subjects out of the clusters and to present these to the employees as a proposal.

When setting up a target agreement, it is useful to shape it after certain criteria, in order to clearly formulate the statements and to avoid misunderstandings or even impossibilities once they have to be put into practice. As reference point the S.M.A.R.T. criteria have proven successful. Targets should have certain characteristics as pointed out below.

**S** specific
**M** measurable
**A** achievable
**R** realistic
**T** terminated

**Figure 9** S.M.A.R.T. Criteria for Target Agreements

Before the executive introduces to the employees the concrete target agreement, it makes sense to have the criteria presented by the moderator to the plenum. This not only works as a reminder to the employees, but will also induce the executive to stay within this quality frame, thereby keeping a certain quality standard for the whole event.

Then the executive will explain the reasons for his choice and prioritization of the presented target agreement and finally ask for the employees' approval.

It is the executive's responsibility to organize the evaluation of the target compliance in the time frame of approximately three months after the workshop (similarly to the review of the Staff Dialogue). The follow-up date for the evaluation should be fixed during the workshop.

The moderator will finally ask the participants on their thoughts to the workshop as a whole and in how far expectations were met, and possibly receive information on the question in how far upward feedback carried out in form of a feedback workshop is accepted. Then it is up to the executive to close up the workshop.

After all, it is the executive who invited to the workshop and it is him who should close it up, thanking the employees for their participation.

Ideally, an invitation should now follow for an excursion, a common lunch or dinner, etc. in order to place the workshop within an agreeable and worthy frame. This terminates the process of the upward feedback which may start again after one year's time.

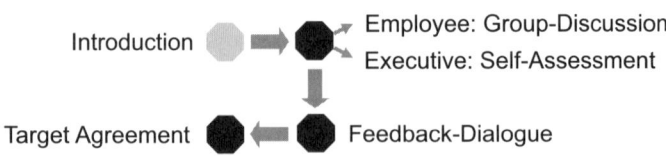

**Figure 10** Upward Feedback as Moderated Workshop

*The Role of the Moderator*

The role of the moderator may, depending on the situation and the participants, make high demands to his ability to deal with different imponderabilities. Additionally to the normal rules of moderation which always have to be complied with, the moderator in the course of the upward feedback process must pay special attention to the fact that feedback is given in an atmosphere of esteem. The moderator's role is a protective one towards employees as well as towards the executive.

The stronger the impression is which the personality of the moderator makes in comparison to the executive, the more the employees will normally tend to address the feedback to the moderator instead of the executive. In these cases, the moderator has to keep on withdrawing and referring the statements to the executive.

The basic position of the moderator should be one of neutrality, objectivity, coolness and politeness. However, within the setting of an upward evaluation, it is not rare that during the workshop conflicts break up resp. long lasting conflicts come to the surface at this specific occasion.

The method of choice in conflict moderation is here to make the conflict a subject of discussion (see Chapter 2.1.2, TCI) and, if at all possible, to clarify it. If this is not possible, it is the art of the moderator to recognize the point where he has to interrupt the process and fix another date for clarification. Criticism should never be understood by the moderator as a personal attack; he is well advised to follow the structure of the workshop in a polite and firm manner. Experienced moderators know that certain employee roles can be found in almost any group-dynamic setting and that there are tactics to keep them under control successfully.

## 2.4 360° Feedback

While the staff dialogue is carried out top-down and the complementary upward feedback bottom-up, the 360-degree feedback extends these processes additionally to colleagues (the Peer Group), clients, superior executive and, if need be, further participants. The concept of the 360-degree feedback was already developed in the 1970s by the American Psychologist Clark Loudon Wilson (1914-2006) and is applied today worldwide, mostly in an electronic form, in enterprises within the frame of executive evaluations (so-called Management Audits resp. Leadership Appraisals).

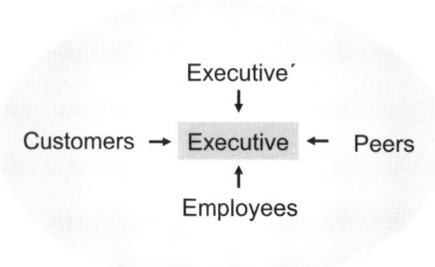

**Figure 11** 360° Feedback

In cases where a 360-degree feedback process is carried out in addition to the upward feedback, the results can be successfully used in the upward feedback. They can be brought together with the anonymous results from the employees' side and included into the feedback dialogue.

It is the moderator's responsibility that in this process no attempt is made to assign the anonymous feedback to certain persons. On the contrary, the opportunity should be seized to make the often standardised form of the feedback by questionnaires more transparent to the executive by giving examples and explanations and by giving him the possibility to ask the authors questions as to comprehension, if needed.

The advantage of the 360-degree evaluation consists in the possibility to have the person in question evaluated from all essential perspectives within the organization and to enable, especially by means of electronics, a questioning and evaluation even on an international basis within a very short time frame. The 360° Feedback is mostly used in the evaluation of executives, but its application also makes sense for project leaders and other key functions in the enterprise.

If the executive to be evaluated does not have any disciplinary direction over employees, the area "employees" is left open or can be completed by other relevant persons concerned. It may be helpful to compare the results from the 360-degree evaluation with the results of a self-evaluation that refers to the same criteria, so that the superior executive (executive') can be offered further information on the evaluated executive and in that way help him in his decision concerning the further personal development of the evaluated manager.

For all performance management systems a principle applies that is also valid for the 360° evaluation: It is a must that the evaluated criteria are in agreement with the existing management guidelines resp. the general competency model of an enterprise. External criteria as they often come from management consultants from outside a company should never be taken over without examination.

## 2.5 Human Resources Controlling

Controlling in general normally means a comprehensive controlling instrument for the profit-oriented, entrepreneurial activities of an enterprise. Human resources controlling focuses on the strategic targets that especially refer to the personnel in an enterprise resp. the applied processes in personnel management.

Controlling refers here to the analysis of past processes as well as to the deduction of suitable measures and the prognosis resp. the future-oriented planning. It has to be clear that this analysis – like any kind of analysis – does not have inherent its decision criteria. Controlling therefore has to be seen solely as support to the management. To deduct conclusions from the analysed data will always remain a task reserved to the management.

Approximately since the 1990s, many enterprises have adopted a thinking which besides the purely quantitative performance indicators includes also qualitative ones. Very often, the responsible persons in personnel management themselves were not interested in encouraging this thinking, for example by reasoning that personnel work consisted for the most part of qualitative elements and could not be compared in one breath with quantitative performance indicators.

Nowadays there is no question that all personnel processes like any other processes are subject to a detailed controlling, and instruments like the balanced score card are excellently suitable for also deducting qualitative key performance indicators (KPIs). Depending on the organization of an enterprise, this controlling can be evaluated by the responsible persons in the personnel management or from other sides in the enterprise, for instance from quality management side.

Like in quality assurance where demands have to be met that beforehand are to be defined, controlling in itself has no meaning before it is filled with concrete substantial target instructions. Hereunder, we will describe the concrete deduction of performance indicators by using the balanced score card, which is one possible instrument in personnel controlling.

### 2.5.1 Balanced Score Card

The balanced score card (BSC) was designed at the beginning of the 1990s by Robert Kaplan, Professor at Harvard Business School, and David Norton, President of the consulting firm Renaissance Solutions, Inc.

Their achievement was to put at the disposal of the executives an instrument which measures the activities of an enterprise by criteria allowing an approach beyond a purely financial frame (like the Du Pont System of Financial Control or the later-on developed ZVEI Performance Measurement System).

Although the criteria have to be adapted individually to each enterprise, they propose an approach which additionally to the inevitable financial perspective also takes into consideration the perspectives of at least the employees, the clients and the processes.

These perspectives, of course, can be extended to any further stakeholders relevant to an enterprise, like suppliers, society, politics etc. In this way, the balanced score card bears in mind not only the shareholder value but also the stakeholder value which, in turn, will be of benefit to the shareholders as well.

The balanced score card breaks down often rather vaguely formulated targets and models to at least four perspectives and from there deduces concrete quantitative performance indicators or qualitative measures.

In those cases where performance indicators cannot be formulated, it is important to apply a comparable qualitative standard as can be found for example in a package of measures or in S.M.A.R.T. target agreements (see Chapter 2.3.1). Reaching the target agreements has back coupling effect on the original targets resp. will be part of the new strategy formulation.

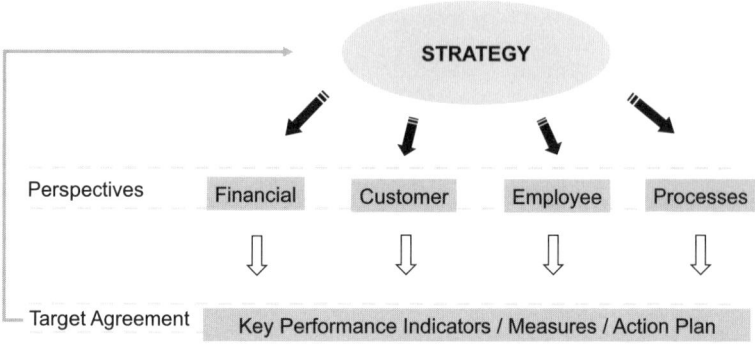

**Figure 12** Deduction of Target Agreements according to the BSC

In the BSC, targets are pursued in a balanced way, i. e. it is permanently evaluated what effects measures have on all targets. Therefore, when putting it into realistic practice, not too many performance indicators at a time should be looked at.

A guide number would be one to two performance indicators per perspective; a total of not more than 20 key performance indicators should be used. This is an important point which, at the same time, demonstrates the weak spot of this instrument: making the mistake of using too many targets at a time, too complex ones or even completely wrong ones does not prevent from the possibility of their being put into practice in a professional and competent way. Because, as is usual with controlling instruments, the content of the targets is not subject to examination.

While performance indicators can be clearly determined numerically, target agreements should be made following the S.M.A.R.T. principle and concrete measures should be described in a detailed package of measures, specifying measure, responsible person and date.

If for any reasons, these criteria are not sticked to – for instance because the criterion "achievable" in the S.M.A.R.T. principles is not achieved – this has to be responded to by an allocation to one's own responsibility or from outside.

If the criteria of the balanced score card are used within a staff dialogue, unexpected divergences may be taken into account by stating the reasons for the target deviation. Whereas the original design by Kaplan and Norton does not allow for any risk management concerning the putting into practice of target agreements, this design may well be extended by the introduction of risks.

## 2.5.2 Performance Indicators for Human Resources Management

Following are a few examples for performance indicators in human resources management. On the level of the strategy, we will mostly find only general, unspecific descriptions like for instance the target to establish a competitive recruiting within the enterprise. This very vague description has to be broken down to concrete possible perspectives, so that clear activities can be defined.

On the financial side, the target could for example be to reduce costs regarding the employment of new staff. If these costs are considered to be not competitive, a consequence could be to outsource parts of the job. Especially for smaller companies it may be advisable in economically busy peak periods not to build up an own special recruiting department, but to transfer this job to an external personnel consultant.

Another possible answer to this challenge could be to delegate to external services parts of the personnel recruiting that take much time, for instance the preselection of candidates. If this, let's say for personnel marketing reasons, is not advantageous, one may think of other solutions to cut costs like debiting these costs to other departments within the company. Instead of having to work with an internal allocation account, personnel departments could charge their services directly to the responsible departments. This ensures a better justified allocation of costs in the enterprise and, at the same time, makes more transparent the services provided.

On the level of the customer perspective, the justification would be an increased contentment of the applicants. An activity deduced therefrom could be interviews, held with employed candidates and refused candidates.

Even if the recruiting process, strictly speaking, finishes with the signing of the working contract, the integration phase often as well is considered as part of the recruiting process. The contentment of recently hired staff can be increased and possible unintended fluctuation during the trial period avoided with an integration program which especially supports network building.

Competitive recruiting on the level of the processes can be reflected in the performance indicators of "time to fill", resp. "time to hire". If the process until signing of the working contract, resp. the actual taking up of work, takes too much time, it could be considered to introduce an electronic handling of the applications.

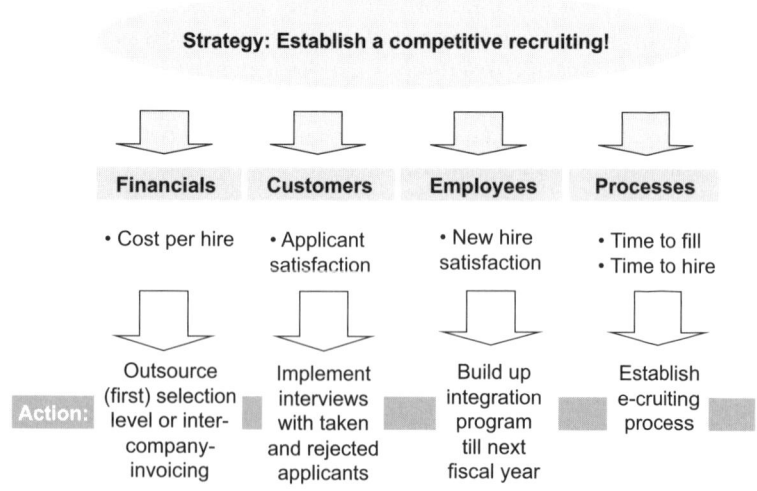

**Figure 13** Deduction of HR Performance Indicators according to BSC

All outlined measures have to be further specified and when concretely put into practice, they will have to be formulated in further milestones and packages of measures, stating the responsible persons and the dates or directly the quantitative performance indicators.

Reasonable performance indicators for successful personnel work could be, as far as recruiting is concerned, the already mentioned factors "time to fill" and "time to hire" and also the costs per employee hired. Furthermore may be examined the ratio between employment contract offers and signed contracts. How many interviews take place until an employee is hired? How content are recently hired employees? What is the fluctuation rate during the trial period? What is the correlation between the results of the assessment process and the later success in the enterprise?

When further evaluating these performance indicators, one will have to find out the qualitative reasons, for example the reasons for a high fluctuation during the trial period or the indicated causes for the refusal of applicants. Finding out the reasons is not only necessary in order to be able to successfully prevent problems, but moreover the result can directly be used as feedback for the strategy, and it can produce new strategies and target definitions, which in their turn, are broken up by means of the balanced score card into new target agreements.

Performance indicators for a successful personnel marketing could be the number of qualified applications received or the ranking of an enterprise in a list of popular employers. Here, in order to be able to interpret the indicators precisely, the next step would be to qualitatively evaluate for example the reasons stated for applications submitted. This procedure also helps clarify the responsible parties. Obviously, a personnel marketing department may not solely be held responsible for the overall image of an enterprise, the so-called employer branding.

The success of a personnel department that inhouse pursues a socially acceptable separation management may for instance be measured by a defined placement ratio (e. g. > 80 %) within a defined period of time (e. g. 9-12 months). On the other hand, the relapse ratio of former employees who, after a successful placement, are being dismissed during the trial period could be a relevant performance indicator for outplacement.

The time has long gone when personnel development departments were limited essentially to the responsibility for the continued learning process of the employees and where it was refused to deduce from a purely qualitatively described work also quantitative performance indicators. today, on the contrary, modern human resources management is challenged with extensive responsibilities.

Not only the number of trainings or their costs but also the design and implementation of employee interviews and organizational development processes, as well as performance management instruments including the methods to measure their success are now day-to-day business. How high is the employees' contentment? What is the fluctuation rate? How far do predictions made by means of personnel development instruments concerning the potential of an employee match later on the actual career made in the enterprise? What are the reasons for qualified employees to leave the enterprise? What is to be learned from these results? What measures are to be taken in order to improve the situation? In how far have these measures been successful?

An active personnel department will certainly not wait until from the side of controlling or quality management it is called for a proof of successful personnel work in the form of performance indicators. It will, on the contrary, on its own initiative define concrete indicators and issue regular reports.

On the level of the department reporting, the responsible executives are well advised to make their contribution already at the early stage when the strategy is formulated and to make available their expert know-how, helping in that way to create positive expectations towards personnel management performance.

# Chapter 3

# Coaching as Instrument of Executive Development

In the following, we do not intend to give a general introduction into coaching, but we will present coaching as the superlative in executive development. Coaching is more expensive and takes more time than the usual training seminars, but the increase in value consists in the fact that executives and key personnel of an enterprise get a made-to-measure package for their specific problems or their development requirements.

This presumes that the normal training contents that refer to the personality development – and not to specialized competencies –, like communication analysis, presentation, (conflict) moderation, or standard management trainings have already been gone through. While a standard training, comparable to a watering can, pours out the contents of a certain seminar or training goal to a whole group of employees or executives, coaching as an individual measure directly focuses on the starting position of the executive in question, the coachee.

Contrary to a trainer, the coach therefore will not be in a position to define from the beginning the goal of the coaching. It will be developed during the course of the development measure. At the end, the coachee will have to define himself the goal, and the role of the coach is to consult and support during that process.

Like there is a dividing line between coaching and training, there is another one concerning therapeutic measures. Although many coaches are studied therapists and often carry out this profession simultaneously, coaching focuses on the personal development of the executive which is relevant to the job function and the enterprise. Personal concerns may be affected, but they should not become the main subject of the sessions. In such a case, it is a matter of ethics and professionalism on the part of the coach to break up the coaching with an executive as soon as it becomes clear that the sessions are dominated by personal contents, resp. that the coachee is actually in need of a therapy.

While the dividing line between the role of a coach from that of a therapist or trainer always has been relatively clear, during the last years a new trend has come up which consists in a twofold role of executive and coach. In these cases, the job profile of an executive includes the function of a coach for the employees.

The question must be allowed if it is possible to fill out this twofold role without conflict of interests. On the one hand the executive is supposed to give advice to his employees, on the other hand he has to evaluate them as superior. Is it not expected too much from employees to reveal weak points while knowing that later on these will be used by the executive for the performance evaluation?

In many enterprises, however, the twofold role of executive and coach is not as extensively defined as is done in professional coaching. The twofold role of a coaching executive is rather understood as consulting and mentoring of the employee within the personal development, i. e. discussion of individual development paths within the enterprise, advice on further steps to go, etc.

This is nothing less than the actual task of an executive anyway. A training program that trains executives as coaches for their employees aims at supporting and strengthening the executive in his function to develop the personality of his employees.

He is not asked to take on the role of a professional coach, which is the reason why the term in a narrow sense should only be used for development measures that take place with an external, neutral, professional coach outside the enterprise.

Coaching in the enterprise principally may be used as preventive measure in the personal development (PD) of executives, or any time when a specific problem or a need for development becomes evident.

Weaknesses in performance on the part of executives or key function personnel (e. g. project manager, sales staff, etc.) may have considerable effects that do not only concern the person in question. A bad performance of an executive may prevent many employees from adequate performance and so present a disturbance of the organizational flow.

If coaching is applied here, it is to be seen as an intervention within the field of organizational development (OD). Coaching in this way can be used in a prophylactic or in a deficit situation.

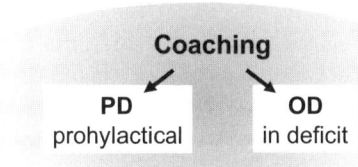

**Figure 14** Coaching: Fields of Application

# 3.1 Quality Criteria and Process Stages

As the term "Coaching" is not protected and as long as no generally applicable training with certification exists in the market, it may be wise for an enterprise to define own quality criteria. These criteria should refer to the required training of coaches as well as to the coaching process itself, as it is in normal cases being implemented and controlled by the personnel department.

Confidentiality between the external coach and the executive as coachee remains guaranteed, as the control by the personnel department is absolutely restricted to the evaluation of the process without disclosure of any session contents.

The task of the personnel department, in its turn, is to define the frame within which professional coaching should take place in the enterprise, thereby protecting the enterprise from excessive costs and the coached executives from dubious coaches.

Now we want to look at possible criteria which an enterprise may apply to the selection of coaches.

*Criteria of Certification*

In case an enterprise intends to tie up the selection of coaches to quality criteria, the obvious thing to do would be for the personnel department to lead certification interviews with external coaches. As recommendable with all selection interviews, a structured interview guideline with open questions should be established. It will ensure comparability and process security and will give instructions as to how the different questions are to be assessed and evaluated.

In order to be able to talk on an equal level with the executives to be coached, a coach should be a university graduate and he additionally should have passed a coaching or supervision training. If there are difficulties in comparing different training certificates, then the contents of the training passed, as well as duration and date of the training have to be closely examined. With regards to intensity, a three-months training finished in one piece may certainly not be compared with a training that was done besides one's job over several years or even with a fulltime training.

Also to be examined is the consulting approach behind the training. Even if the enterprise should not have any preference as to a psychotherapeutic, gestalt therapeutic or family therapeutic direction, the professional experience of the coach should indicate that he is able to transfer therapeutic contents to the economic contents of the everyday work of executives. Although for the consulting job it may on the one hand be very beneficial that the coach is having an objective look from the outside, on the other hand, own experience as executive or knowledge of the trade may also be helpful for the job and may increase acceptance by the executive to be coached.

Further questions to be answered may be: Has the coach an own quality control proved for example by own supervision and continuing training? Are there any references, especially from the charging enterprise? How many years resp. hours of coaching experience can be referred to? Also, individual questions concerning working method and working ethics should be asked. What would the coach consider as conflict (of interests) in his own work? How does he deal with it? How are quality and also success defined in coaching?

Finally, it is important to find out what subjects and what target clientele the coach is best suitable for. Nobody will be able to offer all subjects in the same professional way and furthermore, there will always be preferences as to the group of possible clients. As is usual in the services sector, the coach should be in a position to indicate and explain his own USP (Unique Selling Proposition).

## Process Criteria

As soon as the personnel department has certified enough coaches for a coaching pool, coaching work can be started with. The question how many coaches should be contained in a pool depends on a variety of factors, like size of the enterprise, distribution of the locations, main consulting topics, acceptance in the enterprise, etc.

The engagement of a coach may be justified by prophylactic or deficit requirements, as we have already seen. In both cases, it makes sense if this indication is made by the personnel department on the part of the responsible person attending to the executive in question. In cases where the decision comes from the direct superior of the potential coachee, the personnel expert will be in the same dilemma as is a coach who is being "prescribed" to a coachee. In both cases, the personnel expert as well as the coach will try within the three-way relation of 1) superior executive, 2) potential coachee and 3) coach to clarify the assignment, to make it transparent or, if need be, to reject it.

The personnel expert must be in a position to recognize if on the basis of the described situation there is a coaching need or if other measures are to be advised. Here, internal or external trainings, promotion programs or similar measures could be considered. In each individual case the expert from the personnel department also has to recognize where the limit has to be set, i. e. where personal topics and problems start, meaning that reference should be made to the social services of the enterprise where, if need be, external therapeutic help can be recommended.

Here again the question has to be asked if confidentiality of coaching, which we saw in danger already in the cases of the twofold role of an executive as coach, is not also hurt in the relation between personnel expert and coachee. After all, the personnel department does play a part in the performance evaluation of executives.

This problem can be controlled by limiting and prioritizing the problem presentation during the indication phase. The personnel expert does not have to learn more than a few key features from the potential coachee in order to be able to choose a suitable coach from the coach pool. In reality, it may of course happen that by describing concrete problem examples also certain contents are transferred, however, this can be tolerated within the confidentiality that personnel experts have to keep.

As soon as the personnel expert has found out from the executive the topics and problems to be treated, he must be in a position, based on his know-how and experience, to decide what professional measures are suitable as remedy. They range from professional to personal trainings in the enterprise, from in-company promotion measures to cooperation with universities and training organizations from the outside.

If the personnel expert discovers problems in the personal field that are not relevant to the everyday working situation resp. that go beyond the scope of the described measures, he should recommend to the executive a suitable contact within or outside the enterprise.

Contacts within the enterprise may be social counseling or medical services which, after further indication, may, if need be, assure transfer, for example, to external therapeutic services.

Once the personnel expert has come to the conclusion that coaching would be a reasonable measure to help the executive, he will choose from the coaching pool two to three coaches suitable for the topics in question and present their profiles to the executive.

This presentation should contain curriculum vitae, photo, references, internet address of the homepage and fees. With this information, the executive is put in a position to get a good picture of the hard and soft facts and it will enable him to choose his coach. The choice does not need any explanation and should not be questioned.

It is also to be accepted if executives, without including questions of qualification, make their choice with a preference for a certain age, sex, etc. Furthermore, the possibility should be given that the executive has a meeting with all recommended coaches, without costs and obligation, to find out about the necessary personal liking.

The possibility of a first talk without costs and obligation has to be included by the personnel department – besides questions to further process stages – into the certification interviews with the potential coaches. After a first talk, the executive should make his decision for a certain coach.

On principle, there is of course the possibility that none of the coaches meets with approval; practically, however, this case does not occur, on condition that competent preparation and steering by the personnel expert was given. The choice between two to three suitable coaches represents a good value, as the options in the coaching pool are of a finite nature.

Although each coach will apply a different methodical approach, certain process stages should be defined as quality criteria that may not be missing in any coaching. They enable the personnel expert as well as the executive to make transparent the status and the progress of the sessions without mentioning confidential contents.

Process controlling is inevitable because it can avoid possible delaying tactics or time extensions by dubious coaches. It is applied to all six process stages: 1) first talk, 2) diagnosis, 3) development, 4) transfer, 5) evaluation and 6) conclusion.

Hereunder, we will explain the stage components while the concrete contents of the applied methods remain in the field of the individual working method of the coach.

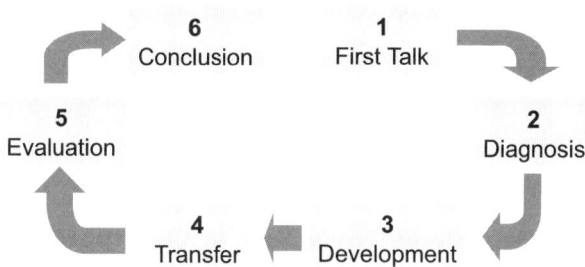

**Figure 15** Coaching Stages

In the first talk, the coach will, on the basis of descriptions of exact situations, once more define and specify the topic or topics and take down on record a concrete target agreement. Moreover should be discussed general subjects concerning coaching, like confidentiality or rules to be applied in the case the coaching is broken off. All this should be taken down in writing in a "contract" as agreement between coach and executive.

Before passing to the diagnosis stage, the actual position of the executive will be defined, covering all fields from available competences up to analysis of past attempts to solve the problems and existing resources. At this stage already, methods of problem analysis as well as methods of reflection will be applied as basis for the analysis of and confrontation with self-image vs. outside image.

Following this are concrete development models with solution scenarios which may find their expression in methods of confrontation, in trial actions or in role training.

In the transfer phase the executive will try to implement and train in daily routine what has been learnt. During that time, the coach may function as escorting shadow, if desired, or give his support only by telephone advice.

Finally, coach and coachee should measure the overall success of their actions by comparing the original target (if it has not been newly defined in the course of the coaching) with the status quo and the satisfaction on the part of the coachee with the result reached.

At this point, it may make sense to include into the considerations relevant records taken earlier, records concerning the outside image or generally relevant feedback that in the meantime has come up from the enterprise.

The demands should not be exaggerated so that the executive does not needlessly get under pressure. In cases where coaching comes across deeper, personal subjects, progress may often only reasonably be assessed after several months.

After this evaluation, coaching will end with the conclusion stage in which for the coachee it should become clear what benefit was provided by the coaching, what points may have been left open and what are the perspectives of further development for the executive.

Furthermore, a good close may be the deepening of the learning matter resp. discussing how it can be transferred to future situations on one's own authority.

## Coaching Evaluation

While the coach is subject to controlling by the personnel expert as well as by the coached executive with regards to the transparency of the process status, it is also advisable for the personnel expert to undergo himself a quality control process by measuring and recording the respective success of a coaching measure and by making it then part of future recommendations.

With this feedback of measured success regarding the future choice of coaches as well as possibly the criteria of certification themselves, the cycle of the process control is closed.

For the evaluation of coaching, different ways may be chosen. Especially for mid-term and long-term evaluations it will be useful to include conclusions from performance management results gained in the enterprise (Upward Feedback, 360° Evaluation) as well as direct feedback from superior executives or other relevant persons.

As in most cases, for confidentiality reasons, this approach will not be chosen, it is recommendable to take as a basis for the evaluation the assessment by the executive. For obvious reasons, a two-stage approach

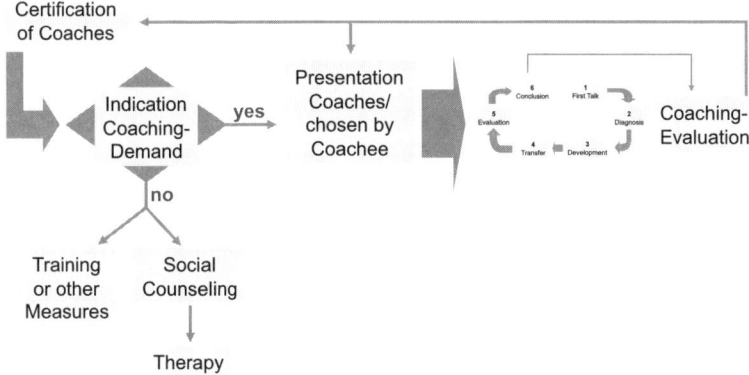

**Figure 16** Steering the Coaching Process

which combines the impression directly after the coaching with a mid-term impression set up after a few months, would be the most valid one. For practical reasons, however, in most cases one single evaluation after the coaching will have to suffice.

The method of choice may here be a confidential questionnaire measuring the satisfaction of the coachee by just a few criteria that, in their turn, become then part of the evaluation of the coach in the coaching pool. Was the frequency of the appointments appropriate? Were concrete coaching targets given? Was it possible to transfer the experiences made during coaching into daily routine and have concrete possibilities of action been gained for the daily routine? Has the executive gained more consciousness concerning own strengths and weaknesses and does he see his situation in general clearer than before? After each process stage has there been a common résumé with discussion how to proceed further? Did the executive have the impression that the coach was sure of himself and professional at all times? Would the executive give the coach a recommendation? Was coaching more effective than training could have been?

Answers to these and similar questions on the questionnaire, in addition to a field for free remarks of the executive, can be assessed corresponding to their significance. They may be a good basis for the evaluation of the coach in the coaching pool.

## 3.2 Consulting Approaches

With qualitative criteria and process stages we have presented the form in which coaching should be carried out. Now the time has come to describe in more detail some of the contents, i. e. basic consulting approaches.

It is useful for the executives undergoing a coaching as well as for the personnel department that places the coaching orders to know and to understand the basic consulting approaches in order to be able to assess these approaches adequately. We are presenting in the following four consulting approaches which are quite common. This selection, however, does not represent an evaluation with regards to those approaches not mentioned.

*Psychotherapy*

Coaches with a psychotherapeutic education normally work simultaneously in their own psychotherapeutic practice. For an enterprise, it may be useful to have in their coaching pool a mixture of rather business-oriented coaches as well as a certain number of coaches who are in a position to deal with deeper and more complex subjects, if need be.

Honest coaches will not take advantage of the coaching to generate own therapy sessions following the coaching. While psychotherapy often is used as a generic term for all therapeutic methods, we will use it here only in a more limited sense. We are talking about psychoanalytic (developed by Sigmund Freud, Carl Gustav Jung or Alfred Adler) and behavior therapeutic (developed from Behaviorism after Edward Thorndike, J. B. Watson, and B. F. Skinner) methods.

Contrary to – or additional to – methods that are meant to enhance personal development, the concern and the target of psychotherapy are to reach recovery for patients in their mental or physical suffering or at least to arrive at some relief. The causes and the connections the patient will learn about during his therapy should help giving a push to his own personal development and possibly changing his own personality structure.

Analytically oriented psychotherapy also focuses on the confrontation with the patient's unconscious for the explanation of the causes of behavior and suffering.

Without any doubt, personal life problems and the behaviour within the working environment have a strong connection. However, it cannot be the task of an enterprise or the task of a coaching measure, organized and paid by the employer, to treat principal life problems of their executives. This would definitely go beyond the scope of enterprise activities as regards cost and time. Moreover, apart from very few serious cases, behaviour in work and behaviour in private life can very well be treated separately and successfully.

Especially as regards the use of coaches with psychotherapeutic approach, the responsible persons will have to consider very carefully in how far the solution of personal problems is necessary and reasonable for a successful change of professional behavior.

*Psychoanalysis*

Unlike behaviour therapy which attempts to change behaviour by training, the purpose of psychoanalysis is to uncover the mostly unconscious causes and to make the patient understand the connections behind his suffering. As causality research sometimes goes very far into the past, psychoanalysis is a past-oriented method which quite frequently deals with (early) childhood experiences.

Psychoanalysis may take very much time and be long-drawn-out, up to several hundred sessions. In the classical psychoanalysis after Freud, the patient lies on a sofa and talks without any censorship and freely associating about everything in his mind. The analyst, sitting behind him, listens and interprets to the patient the findings having come up during the session.

A special effort will be made by the analyst to find out the projections of emotional patterns of the patient which will come up in the relationship between patient and analyst. He has to interpret their importance and make them accessible for change. Furthermore, the analysis of dreams which may be an alternative access to the unconscious of the patient, will be a subject during the analytical treatment.

*Behavior Therapy*

In the 1950s, in the USA, behaviourism – based especially on experimentally developed learning theories – came up as a forerunner of the subsequent behavior therapy. As a result of their dissatisfaction with the poor effectiveness of depth psychological methods, the behavior therapists greatly stress the importance of empirical verification of their methods. Here it is vital to acquire an exact behavior analysis to define the actual determinants of the behavior.

Contrary to the prevalent credo in psychoanalysis, for the achievement of change in behavior it is not considered as absolutely necessary to find out the causes of the problems. This view has especially proven successful when dealing with compulsive behaviour or with phobia, and in certain cases it results in a shorter therapy duration. Unlike in psychoanalysis, the focus here is on learning resp. forgetting certain behaviour patterns without denying for example genetic factors. The change of the problematic behavior has priority, not its explanation.

Behavior therapy works with methods that, for example, are based on the theory of classic conditioning and attempts to establish a counter conditioning for instance by exposition. These methods are often applied in cases of phobia, panic or obsessive disorders.

The patient exposes himself to the problematic stimuli, at first only in his imagination then in reality in a gradual way, hereby reaching systematically a desensitization.

Psychoanalysts accused behavior therapy of essentially only reducing or eliminating the symptoms instead of removing the cause of disorders, and that this could lead to the development of new symptoms (with the same cause), the so-called symptom shifting.

More criticism came and is still coming from representatives of other directions like humanist psychology or gestalt therapy. They complain about the coupling to a behavioral idea of man that sees man strongly dominated by his environment as stimulus-reaction system.

## Transactional Analysis

Transactional analysis was founded by the Canadian psychiatrist Eric Berne (1910-1970) in order to analyse communication structures. Three states of the ego are to be distinguished; each of them being formed in childhood: 1) parent, 2) adult, and 3) child. The parent ego represents feelings, thoughts and actions as conveyed by the parents as former authorities. They have been taken over by a person into his own parent ego. The parent ego is also called "exteropsyche" by Berne.

The adult ego, also called "neopsyche", focuses on one's own conscious decisions, while the child ego, also called "archeopsyche" refers to experiences and behaviour in childhood.

In the transactional analysis, existing communication patterns are being led back to these ego functions in order to make transparent the interactions in a first step and then subsequently offer possibilities of dissolving the disorder. In this way the expression of the parents ego may be considerate or critical, that of the grown-up ego appropriate and reasonable and that of the child ego well-adapted or rebellious.

The transactional analysis makes a distinction between parallel and cross over transactions. A parallel transaction happens within the same ego state that was originally addressed, whereas in a cross over transaction, the answer comes from a partner in another than the addressed ego state.

Transactional analysis furthermore acknowledges the hidden transaction, meaning that under an open message an additional message (mostly non-verbal) is transported. Although parallel transactions do not cause disturbances and may principally be continued as a "game", the target remains to conduct parallel communication in mutual respect and within the adult ego state.

A collaborator of Eric Berne, Thomas Harris, later called this relationship an approach of "I am okay – you are okay", an expression which later on, as a shortened motto for the transactional analysis, became rather popular and was taken over by other consulting approaches like neurolinguistic programming (NLP) or theme centralized interaction (TCI).

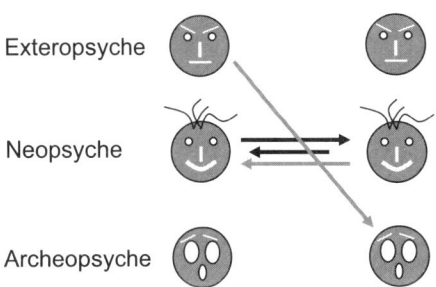

**Figure 17**
Parallel and Cross Over Communication in Transactional Analysis

*Neurolinguistic Programming*

Neurolinguistic Programming (NLP) was founded by the psychologist Richard Bandler and the linguist John Grinder. Bandler and Grinder started by examining therapy approaches by Fritz Perls (Gestalt Therapy), Virginia Satir (Family Therapy) and Milton Erickson (Hypnotherapy) and combined the findings with the ideas from linguistics as well as the analysis of the behavior patterns of outstanding personalities in the field of entrepreneurship, artistry or science.

Accordingly, NLP is not based on a defined scientific theory, but may be understood as a collection of methods aiming at permanent further development (so-called "NLP formats").

A few typical instruments in NLP are "pacing" and "leading". Pacing reflects behaviour patters of the counterpart (for example intonation, posture, etc.). Leading wants to give signals aiming at having the counterpart follow on and join in. The target is not manipulation (and "programming" is not to be understood manipulatively), but the establishment of emotional contacts.

Other typical methods in NLP are autosuggestion, the so-called "anchoring" (which corresponds to the classic Conditioning) as well as "reframing".

In autosuggestion, similar as in autogenic training, positive aspects are repeatedly internalized by affirmative statements and thus get more and more reinforced as time goes by.

Anchoring means to tie new emotional connotations or to use existing ones in order to associate specific stimuli and situations with new sensuous perceptions. Anchoring is based on the theory of the classic conditioning as formulated by the physiologist and physician Iwan Petrowitsch Pawlow (1849-1936).

In Pawlow's experiment, the offer of food as unconditional stimulus is followed by flow of saliva as unconditional reaction. The sound of a bell as neutral stimulus is followed by nothing, as expected. However, if the sound of the bell repeatedly appears in a narrow timely connection with the offer of food, the sound alone will finally bring about the dogs' salivation. This phenomenon was called "conditioning" by Pawlow.

The method of anchoring in NLP is supposed to dissolve the originally negative conditioning and tie it to new positive sensations.

In reframing, coming from the family therapy of Virginia Satis, an event is being given a new interpretation. It gets a new frame and a new meaning (for example, is a glass considered half full or half empty?).

The theory of the so-called "autonomous eyes' movements" in NLP means that thoughts may be deduced from the movement of the eyes. A scientifically proven effect, however, has not been confirmed.

The combination of NLP with esoteric contents as pursued by some services and training institutions has contributed to its reputation as a pseudoscience.

## Systemic Therapy

Since the 1960s different therapeutic institutions have been working on concepts that increasingly also include the systems (family, environment, etc.) outside the client (as symptom bearers of the problem). Family therapy assumes that symptoms only can be understood within the context of all members of a family and that a change can only be brought about within this total context.

Systemic therapy and counselling has developed out of this systemic family therapy and is based – besides different family therapeutic schools – on the system theory which, in great variety, has been formulated interdisciplinarily, among others by concepts from biologists, physicists and philosophers. We will examine the system theory thoroughly in Chapter 7.

Systemic counselling is also called solution-oriented counselling because, contrary to for example psychoanalysis, it does not focus on the past – the origin and development of the problem – but puts special emphasis on a future-oriented solution. This is because the resources to solve a problem are seen as different as those who were bringing it to life.

Systemic counselling, unlike psychoanalysis, is a short-time measure and therefore it is appreciated by enterprises for its efficiency and cost saving.

The systemic counsellor will avoid to formulate solutions or even interpretations for the coachee. He sees the client as the expert who will find the solution on his own. The problem is solved where it was made, in the client system.

One of the most important methods of systemic counselling is circular questioning, where environmental perspectives are being included resp. hypotheses on the point of view of other persons concerned are being outlined by the client himself. The purpose is to make the coachee learn to get involved in a change of perspective within the system and in this way to understand the emotions of the other persons around him.

Another typical approach in systemic counselling is the so-called miracle question: the client imagines that a miracle happens and, in everyday life, he discovers that his problem has disappeared. What exactly would have changed? An analysis of such circumstances would be the basis for further procedure of the client, resp. his further point of view on the problem.

Other methods may be for example scale questions that illustrate differences and progresses, or the paradoxical intervention where the therapist paradoxically recommends exactly the problematic behaviour in question thus provoking a reactance in the client and giving a signal for active change in behavior.

The American therapist Virginia Satir is known as an essential founder of systemic therapy and counselling. Among others, her approaches to family sculpture and family reconstruction were the basis for subsequent developments like family setting or the reflecting team (developed by the Norwegian social psychiatrist Tom Andersen), where the client, by changing his place with the therapist, gets a reflection of the therapy. The purpose is to critically question the procedure and the interventions of the therapist by installing an alternate observing system.

Further developments of the systemic counselling were achieved for example by Insa Sparrer and Matthias Varga von Kibéd in form of the "therapy without audible answers". Here, the therapist asks solution-focused questions and the client shows understanding through nodding that he has answered the question to himself. In this way, the therapist accompanies the client by proposing solutions without ever coming to know the actual problem.

Especially the systemic organization counselling which understands problems occurring in enterprises as problems of complex social systems that cannot be considered separately, has established itself successfully in the field of organizational development and change management. Quite a few coaches are active in this field and enterprises should take care that individual coachings for executives are not misused to generate further organization development projects.

# Chapter 4

# Leadership and Ethics

*"What of what concern to me is the common weal?*
*The common weal...is not my weal."*

Max Stirner (1806-1856) – The Ego and his Own

Do our managers lack morals? "Self-service, corruption, fraud, breach of contract – it seems that no rules are valid any more for the elite...The ethical foundations of economy are crumbling."[1] During the last years, the call for binding moral norms for the economic as well as the political elite in our country has grown louder and louder. On the other side, repeated statements keep emphasising that "those managers who in their enterprises respect values, may count on higher profits."[2] Let's examine on what foundation managers can base their values and moral actions on.

## 4.1 Individual Values

In a first step we can see the field of individual values which are supported by and refer to religion, ethical norms and practical morals. In addition, values specific to the individual enterprise may play a role, as they are for example part of company guide lines. Moreover, there is the field of socially established values. All of these resources for values and convictions should be used by managers in order to substantiate their actions with foundation and stability.

On the level of social value systems, enterprises as well as individual protagonists are exposed to a certain pressure to meet demands and developments from society's side , like for instance to make available

---

[1]  Managermagazin 6/2007

[2]  Harvard Business Manager 1/2006

more part time jobs or to grant conditions for a better work-life balance.

On the enterprise level, each employer will define own values and principles specific to the needs of his enterprise. These will not only serve as an internal moral central thread, but can furthermore have outside effects, like for instance on the employer branding and the marketing strategy against other competitors.

In the globalized world, this positioning has consequences even up to the "global market ethics", even if this latter can only be named theoretically. Executives of an enterprise may orientate themselves on demographic benchmarks or on local and global company guide lines – this will not be enough, however, to do justice to the implications of the decisions that executives individually and concretely have to make in conflict and crisis' situations.

No executive will be able to do without a personal tool that can serve as lighthouse of individual values in a stormy sea. These values may have their foundation in religion, ethics and practical morals.

### 4.1.1 Religion, Ethics and Moral Standards

Religious norms and values offer the advantage of absoluteness. By absoluteness of an action, a behaviour or the attitude towards a behaviour is assessed independently from possible consequences or circumstances.

Therefore, lying or killing, for example, are being assessed as absolutely wrong, even if for instance it is supposed that by the death of one individual the death of many could be prevented. Thus, an action should not be used as means for another purpose, or – to put it in another way – no purpose can justify the means employed.

That is the reason why lying and killing for example are assessed as unconditionally wrong.

The absoluteness of such norms as they are inherent in religion do create security of choice and assurance for one's own actions. Religion does not limit itself to only describe existing values in a society, but it sets them normatively.

Unlike religious values, the putting of which into practice has a compulsory character (they are therefore called "deontologic", from the

Greek to deon: the duty), ethics offers different answers to fundamental questions.

Ethics, as a fundamental theoretical concept, are to be differentiated from practical morals, i. e. from the respective concrete acting instructions.

Ethics may be determined heteronomously – for instance by religious commandments – as well as autonomously (by each human being himself), and here again formally (Kant's Categorical Imperative), materially (Max Scheler's Objective Value Ethics), or relatively (for example Utilitarianism).

In an extreme case, ethical relativism allows to break up with all moral standards. Good and evil also become relative. If ethics are not understood in absolute validity but relatively, justification, at the end, is postponed to another finality.

Utilitarianism, for instance, sets as purpose the usefulness of an action for an individual or for society. In the same way, consequentialism assesses the value of an action purely with regards to its consequences. The following story explains very well where the extreme attitude of a subjective consequentialist hypothetically may lead to:

*Uncle Charles, an elderly rich bachelor, and Frederick, his nephew and only heir, are sitting in a small boat, fishing. The waters are full of sharks. No other boat is around. The following dialogue takes place:*

Frederick: *You know, for anything in the world, I have to come into the possession of half a million Dollar, in order to spend them for my pleasure.*

Uncle Charles: *I know you well enough to belief you. Lately, you have made several attempts to come to money which all seem to have failed.*

Frederick: *That's right. Meanwhile, I have come to the conclusion that the only possibility for me to get money is to kill you.*

Uncle Charles: *I am afraid that with your limited talents and your penchant for idleness you indeed have no other possibility to come to money.*

Frederick: *Since you admit that for me there is no other possibility to come to money: what is your advice?*

Uncle Charles: *Since your only wish is to come to money quickly and there is no other possibility for you than to kill me, you should throw me out of the boat.*

Frederick: *I agree with both premises as well as with your conclusion. As I always follow the good advice of my uncle, I will now throw you out of the boat. (Frederick throws Uncle Charles out of the boat).* [1]

This fictitious example, setting a consequentialist attitude against the deontologic commandment "You shall not kill", demonstrates how careful one should be when setting relative values. This could lead, in its turn, to a justification based on pure intellectual ethics, on individual or social usefulness or, just as well, on the values existing in a society.

In the latter case, one would have to describe as good everything that is. On the other hand, from the representatives of an ethical relativism comes the argument that all norms and values – as all the different religions – developed in dependence of their time and culture, can be explained by their conditions of origin and that therefore they have necessarily to be understood only as relative.

After the description of the individual justification of values, we will now examine the values set up by enterprises.

## 4.2 Company Values

Every company has own role models that work in the sense of a "code of conduct". The values that for example are subsumed under corporate responsibility do not represent any financial or entrepreneurial, but an ethical responsibility.

This imperative of values may possibly deal with fair competitor relations, or the safeguarding of the respect toward the dignity of the employees. No matter how the company role model is defined, it has to be deduced, in its turn, from a superior vision (meaning the self image of a company in the future) and a mission (meaning the business assignment that has to be understandable by all customers). The company role model, by the description of the internal cooperation, finally forms the so-called company culture.

While role models for executives do not offer an entirely adequate and concrete enough basis for decisions – for that, they are too generally

---

[1]  R. M. Hare, 1985

formulated – the decisions of an executive have, in their value system, yet to be in accordance with the code of ethics and conduct of an enterprise.

Individual value systems of executives as well as the entrepreneurial responsibility are for their part embedded into the socially imparted value consensus. We therefore now want to see how society values are conveyed.

## 4.3 Society Values: Demography, Part-Time Work and Empowerment

When we now, as third cornerstone, examine society values, we have to distinguish between many different factors. One actual factor in Germany, for instance, is the demographic development. The German population becomes older and older and there is less and less qualified manpower.

The old age quotient (showing – in per cent – the relation of people in the retirement age older than 60 years, to the population in employable age from 20 to 59 years) was 1995 at a rate of 37, 2001 at a rate of 44 and will climb until 2030 to 71, and until 2050 to 78.

While this development is advantageous for employees, for the enterprises it means an increasing competition for the best talents. Enterprises may react in different ways to this situation. One important way will have to be to understand what values are supported by these best talents and what values they want to see realized, just and exactly on their jobs.

For example, a general social trend to a better work-life balance can be made out that plays an increasing role especially with male employed persons with good income. This was convincingly demonstrated among others by the surprisingly great number of men taking advantage of the possibility to stay at home instead of their wives for a certain time after a baby was born.

A further focus will be put on the possibility of flexible part-time and working time models thereby activating the large field of highly qualified women for the enterprises.

It is interesting to observe that in many cases, the decision to work part-time does not necessarily mean a set-back in the career, even if this prejudice is permanently repeated. One could rather speak about a slowed-down career which by no means has to lead to a standstill or even a downward trend.

Because of the economic pressure that the demographic development in Germany will bring about, it is to be expected that the conditions for employees will still have to improve if an enterprise wants to offer competitive and attractive jobs, especially also for qualified women.

A further social trend to which enterprises will have to react is the generally increased importance that is being attached to family values as well as values relevant to contacts at work. Mostly mentioned here are responsibility, confidence and respect[1].

This means that enterprises and their executives should develop a certain sensitivity for the moral and ethical preferences of their employees. Especially the demand to grant to the employees more professional responsibility, the so-called "empowerment"[2] will have to be met in order to gain and to keep highly qualified talents.

Quite substantial changes will have to take place, not only in company culture but also especially in classical leadership. Highly qualified employees who are in a position to choose between employers will make their choice particularly dependent on the empowerment that is granted to them in their field of responsibility.

Such a demographic development does not only take place in Germany, but also in many other countries, and it is not restricted to the highly developed countries.

In the following chapters, we will outline how these new parameters affect personnel management, and how leadership may be understood that is able to meet these challenges. Before, however, we want to look closer at some classical theories of leadership and see what answers we can find there.

---

[1] Cp. e. g. interview with 500 qualified employees and executives, Institut für angewandtes Wissen iaw, Cologne, 2007

[2] The American sociologist Julian Rappaport has established the term empowerment. Originally coming from social psychology, the term is increasingly being used in management when referring to employee motivation.

# Chapter 5

# Theories of Leadership

*"If you have assumed any character beyond
your strength, you have both demeaned yourself ill that,
and quitted one which you might have supported."*
Epictetus[1]

Young employees, when asked what kind of career they would prefer, usually mention as one of the most attractive an executive career, and this irrespective of the fact that for example they dispose of pronounced abilities as experts or project leaders. The reasons are probably neither the additional projects with which young potential executives have to prove their worth nor with the additional work that comes along with the executive career.

In many enterprises nowadays successful alternative career paths in the function of experts or project leaders are offered, explicitly in order to avoid the risk of loosing a very good expert and maybe get an only average or even bad executive instead. Despite of all this, for many young people the executive career remains the most desirable choice. What is the reason for it?

The attraction or even the aura coming along with the executive functions may have its origin in partially unconscious, anthropological facts that imagine executives as superior.

On many different levels – be it famous leaders like Alexander the Great, or power politics as propagated by Machiavelli, or evolutionary biological concepts like for instance the social darwinistic dominance of the stronger, or the alpha animal of a pack of wolves – everywhere we find attractors that are linked with our image of a leader.

One of the most well-known managers corresponding to this image was Jack Welch, 20 years CEO of General Electric, who, when asked about

---

[1]  Enchiridion or Handbook, transl. by Thomas Wentworth Higginson, first published 1865 (37)

his management philosophy – interestingly enough – gave the following reply: "The objective of any human being must be to gain self-assurance"[1]. This, linked with a charismatic style of leadership, could just be understood as the end of any objectivisable managerial technique.

Although Welch was said to cultivate social darwinistic methods – for example by establishing employee rankings every year, following which the best 20% were awarded, the average 70% kept, and the worst 10% fired – he will still go down in history as one of the most influential managers of the 20th century. In "Financial Times" surveys, for example, he was several times selected best manager worldwide.

At the same time, up to now, it has not yet been possible to provide empirical evidence on what the characteristics of a leader personality should be resp. what difference there is between successful leaders and less successful ones. Even if general correlations between successful leadership and personality characteristics could be observed, the individual results were so widely scattered that a deduction of general statements is not permissible.[2]

Because of these inadequacies in theories on leadership characteristics and the variance of demanded characteristics depending on the particular situation and working environment, now, in the more recent discussions on leadership, the definition of specific key qualifications has begun.

Although these abilities are defined in a very general way, compared to characteristic feactures they offer the advantage of changeability and capacity for development, and with this they approach the demand of, for instance, F. Malik, Management Zentrum St. Gallen, to understand leadership and management as specific qualifications analogous to the qualification of lawyers or physicians:

> "In a strange way the imagination has come into the world that managers…had to be a cross-breeding of ancient general, Nobel prize winner for physics and television showmaster…The basic problem boils down to the question: How can we enable normal people – after all, we do not dispose of any others – to produce extraordinary achievements?"[3]

---

[1]  Panel discussion with Jack Welch, Manager Magazin 10.10.2001. cp. also Jack and Suzy Welch: Winning, 2005

[2]  cp. e. g. R. M. Stogdill, 1974

[3]  F. Malik, Führen Leisten Leben, 2001, own translation

In Chapter 4 we have already indicated the parameters on which leadership should increasingly be based if it is to meet the existing society values, namely more responsibility for employees (Empowerment), higher demands by and individualization of qualified employees, only some of these elements being work-life balance and flexible working time structures, especially for qualified women. What does this mean with regards to the demands executives have to meet? Let us first examine the phenomenon "employee motivation" since it is one of the most discussed subjects in literature on personnel management.

## 5.1 Employee Motivation

The motivation of employees can be characterised as determinant of many influential factors, like exciting tasks, colleagues in the team, organizational culture or even a "adequate" executive[1], whatever that may mean. Here, often it is not realized that for example the adequate executive is not the motivating executive, and neither can other factors have a motivation leverage effect by themselves. Motivation can only be reached by every employee and every human being for himself. Sports coaches know this. The question is rather how the existing potential of self-motivation can best be roused in an employee.

Porter and Lawler[2], for example, name intrinsic (factors within the person, e. g. fun) as well as extrinsic reward (coming from outside, e. g. payment) as possible approach to influence one's own motivation and the performance depending on it. A multiple feedback of the existing factors results in manifold interdependencies of the different elements with multicausal complexity.

One aspect that is often forgotten in motivation theories is the neglect, and resulting thereof the overrating of rational decisions. Just a thought alone cannot motivate us to an action. What is essential for any motivation as well as any decision in general is the impetus behind, which makes our choice drop into a certain direction.

---

[1]  L. v. Rosenstiel, G. Comelli, 2001
[2]  L. W. Porter, E. E. Lawler, 1968

Pure reasoning cannot do it, as can be shown in the story of "Buridan's Donkey"[1] who dies of hunger in front of two equal heaps of hay because he is not able to make a decision in view of the equality of the two possibilities.

Buridan's parable, when transferred to man – without wanting to make man smarter than he is – shows the impossibility of a rational decision between two equal solutions. From that reason, we cannot expect a basis for choice in front of equal arguments. The decision must come – like any action – out of inclinations and emotions, as this was already explained by David Hume in his ethics.[2]

What can we learn from this? First: Man can only motivate himself, no executive is able to achieve it or should ever try to achieve it for him. Moreover: If man should get motivated, the impetus for it cannot come from reason, but only from his emotions, inclinations and passions.

These facts have enormous implications on the way leadership should function, resp. on the way in which executives should act and understand their own role so that employees may work in a motivated way. Here we come to the role of the executive. In order to be able to understand how an executive leads his employees, we, in a first step, have to understand an executive's idea of man.

## 5.2 Idea of Man

*"Every individual man carries, within himself,*
*at least in his adaptation and destination, a purely*
*ideal man. The great problem of his existence is*
*to bring all the incessant changes of his outer life into*
*conformity with the unchanging unity of this ideal."*

*Friedrich Schiller (1759-1805)[3]*

---

[1] Parable on the absence of freedom of will, erroneously ascribed to the Paris University Principal Johannes Buridan (approx. 1300-1358), the origins of which, however, are at Aristotle (De Caelo).

[2] David Hume, Enquiries concerning human understanding and concerning the principles of morals, Edition 1777, reprinted 1975 by Oxford University Press, New York

[3] Friedrich Schiller, Letters upon the Aesthetic Education of Man, 1795, (New York, Collier, 1910, Harvard Classics)

Under "idea of man" we have to understand the basic anthropological opinion concerning human nature held by someone. Typical positions in history were represented by the philosophers Thomas Hobbes (1588-1679) in England as well as Jean Jacques Rousseau (1712-1778) in France.

While Hobbes made the assumption that man because of his selfishness is a wolf to man (homo homini lupus) and already in his natural state finds himself in a war of all against all (bellum omnium contra omnes), Rousseau's opinion is that man is basically good and only adopts an aggressive and tyrannical behavior through socialization (Environmentalism).

The logical consequence for Hobbes is the necessity of submission under laws (the state as Leviathan, i. e. mortal God). For Rousseau, man should remain as free as he is born, however, Rousseau also postulates a social contract (Contrat Social) to defeat inequalities.

Two ideas of man that keep being quoted in the economic sciences and represent archetypally the pessimistic resp. optimistic view on human nature are the concepts of F. W. Taylor[1] and A. Maslow[2].


## 5.2.1 Taylor

The American engineer F. W. Taylor assumes that a worker has to be controlled in order to achieve performance. Control is being carried out by the superior whose role therefore is that of a watchdog and slave driver. He assumes that a worker follows similar laws as a machine. Taylor is the founder of the theory of scientific management ("Scientific Management", resp. "Taylorism").

Taylor was interested in perfecting the working activity in a mechanistic sense. For this he made, among other things, time studies in order to form the sequence of operations as efficient as possible. These measurements were taken to procure objective production times for exactly defined working procedures and to define a standard of productivity.

Assembly-line work, for instance, as introduced by Henry Ford in the automobile industry, can be understood as direct realization of this idea

---

[1] F. W. Taylor, Principles of Scientific Management, New York, Harper, 1911
[2] A. Maslow, A Theory of Human Motivation, Psychological Review 50, 1943

as well as the productivity increases of the American industry based on the idea of rationalization after the first world war.

Taylor is said to have been the first one to write an overall theory of business economics. In his view, the performance of a worker can only be achieved by force, resp. wages and punishment have to be used as means of education and in order to keep the workers under control.

Otherwise, according to Taylor's idea of man, the workers will avoid work, keep low their performance and productivity and even sabotage work.

In the long term, even within the conditions of production that were normal in Taylor's time, it was shown that the short-term rationalizations reached by force had a negative effect on the workers' motivation. Superiors were seen as enemies and the workers dissociated themselves emotionally more and more from the enterprise, this leading to quality losses and increased sick leave.

We should add that Taylor's idea of man was not really an idea of man, but rather Taylor's idea of a worker. To the educated upper class, he awarded positive features like diligence, sincerity or economy. He had a two-tier society image.

Antipodal to Taylor's pessimistic view of human nature are the statements of the American psychologist Abraham Maslow (1908-1970).


## 5.2.2 Maslow

*"Human nature is not nearly as bad as it has been*
*thought to be. In fact it can be said that the possibilities of*
*human nature have customarily been sold short."*
A. Maslow

Maslow has especially become well-known for his hierarchy of needs that describes motivation. The model has as basis a fundamental character of development that classifies human needs in a hierarchical manner. These needs are set up one above the other and as long as the stages below are not fulfilled, the higher ones cannot be reached. The objective is to reach the highest stage of need fulfilment which is self-actualization. With examples like suicide or eating disorders which put spiritual ideals above physical ones resp. sublimate spiritual needs into physical ones, Maslow earned quite some criticism. However, this criticism does not take proper account of the refinement of the model, as

Maslow not only accepts the direct satisfaction of needs of higher value, but also distinguishes in his model between individual satisfaction of needs and national resp. society recommendations.

The three lower stages of physiological, security and social needs have been characterised as deficit needs. They have a natural limit in their fulfilment, but they keep coming back. The American psychologist Frederick Herzberg (1923-2000)[1] calls these needs in his 2-factor theory "hygiene factors", which are necessary, and the upper stages "motivators", which are the basis of high motivation.

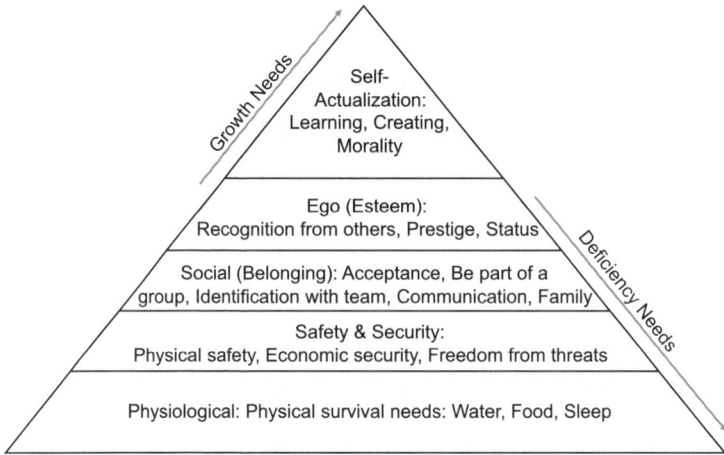

**Figure 18** Hierarchy of Needs by Maslow

The highest stage of self-actualization here is – when understood as individualization – an occidental one. The question turns up if in an Asiatic society the welfare of the group or the community would not be prioritized over that of the individual, with obvious consequences to what a society is ready to accept as adequate conduct.

Maslow with his idea of steadily developing needs represents the belief in growth, educability and changeability of man. Similar for example to the cultural philosophy of the German psychoanalyst Erich Fromm

---

[1] Frederick Herzberg, Work and Nature of Man, London, Crosby Lockwood Staples, 1966

(1900-1980)[1] it is assumed that man has an inherent need for development of the talents within him. This thought, by the way, found its first, preliminary expression by the Greek philosopher and tutor of Alexander the Great, Aristotle (384-322 BC), in his idea of entelechy[2]. According to it, man bears within him the objective of his further development.

### 5.2.3 McGregor

Douglas McGregor (1906-1964), Professor at the Massachusetts Institute of Technology (MIT), takes up the dualistic approach of the optimistic resp. pessimistic idea of man and develops the so-called Theory X resp. Theory Y in which he assigns concrete personnel management methods to these dichotomic ides of man.[3]

McGregor not only describes both positions but explicitly stands up for Theory Y as, in his opinion, not only does it increase employee contentment but it also contributes to a better achievement of company targets.

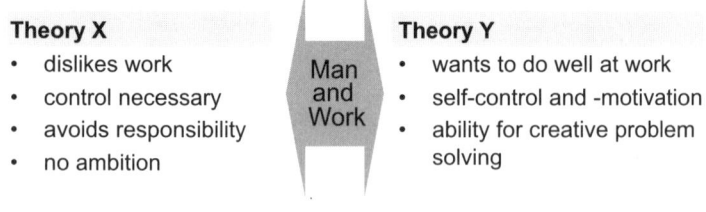

**Theory X**
- dislikes work
- control necessary
- avoids responsibility
- no ambition

Man and Work

**Theory Y**
- wants to do well at work
- self-control and -motivation
- ability for creative problem solving

**Figure 19** Theory X and Theory Y

Depending on the different images of man that are on the basis of Theory X and Theory Y one can deduce consequences for personnel management in each case. Executives bearing an idea of man within them that corresponds to Theory X will understand leadership as an authori-

---

[1] Erich Fromm, Anatomie der menschlichen Destruktivität (1973), Hamburg, Rowohlt, 1991

[2] Aristoteles Metaphysik IX, 8, Hamburg, Meiner, 1991

[3] Douglas McGregor, The human side of Enterprise, New York, 1960

tarian guidance of their employees and management as controlling function. The needs of the employees take a back seat while the executive becomes the focus of attention.

Corresponding to this attitude, the participation of the employees in company decision processes will be small and investments into the development of employee talents will hardly take place. It goes without saying that this kind of idea of man displayed by the executive will lead to a corresponding behavior on the side of the employees, having as a consequence, on the part of the executive, that he feels confirmed in his image of man.

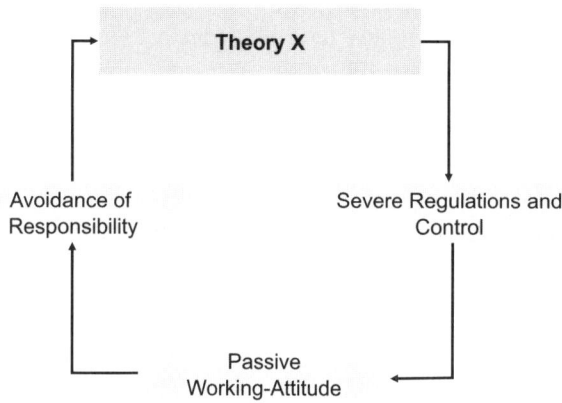

**Figure 20** The Repercussions of Theory X

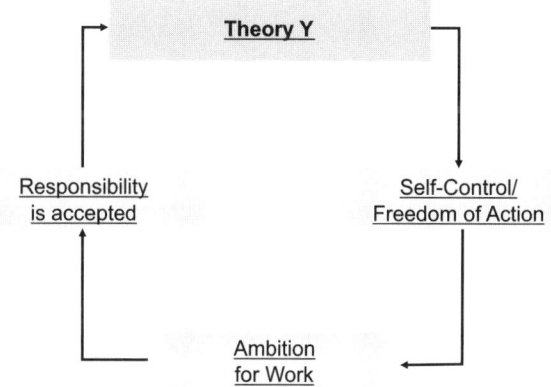

**Figure 21** The Repercussions of Theory Y

Leadership being deduced from Theory Y, on the contrary, will give priority to the motivation of the employees and will strive to gain their commitment. This requires the executive's trust that the employees are achievement-oriented as long as the existing targets and the needs of the employees are compatible. The idea of man of Theory Y will finally have a repercussion in form of a self-fulfilling prophecy on the idea of man of the executive when implemented as personnel management strategy.

## 5.2.4 Schein

A disciple of McGregor and later on also teaching at the MIT, Edgar Schein (*1928), finally postulates four basic ideas of man that can be found on the way of development from "homo oeconomicus" to "homo complexus"[1].

### 1. Rational Economic Man

The rational economic man gets his motivation mostly by monetary incentives. He remains passive and is manipulated and controlled by the organization. He acts rationally and his image of man corresponds essentially to Theory X by McGregor.

### 2. Social Man

The social man is mainly motivated by social needs. Work being more and more experienced as senseless, he is looking for vicarious satisfaction in the form of social relations at his workplace. Correspondingly, social considerations have a greater power than measures of the executive.

### 3. Self-Actualizing Man

The self-actualizing man strives for autonomy and prefers self motivation and self control. The human needs are, similar to the pyramid of Maslow, arranged in a hierarchical way. There is no inevitable conflict between self-actualization and organizational achievement. The image of man essentially follows the Theory Y by McGregor.

---

[1] Edgar H. Schein, Organizational Psychologie, Englewood Cliffs, Prentice Hall, 1980

*4. Complex Man*

The complex man is multi-layered, capable of change and of learning. He differentiates his conduct depending on the situation and his motivation is directed to different targets in different situations.

Like McGregor, Schein also does not consent himself with the conception of these ideas of man but deduces from them concrete consequences for leadership. Regarding the management of the economic man, this means the focus on a structured organization and efficient working processes with strong controlling functions.

For the social man, the requirements will be to set up group incentive systems and to meet the needs for affiliation and identity.

The self-actualizing man is best dealt with if the executive plays the role of a promoter who is prepared to integrate him in his decisions and to delegate responsibilities.

For the complex man, finally, there is no concrete adequate management conduct as there is no generally adequate organization. Here, the executive should be able to diagnose situations and depending on them, adapt a flexible conduct.

As can be seen, Edgar Schein goes already far beyond the description of images of man and presents matching management styles. In basic statements the proposed treatment of the complex man already corresponds to the situative leadership style as formulated by Hersey and Blanchard.

The time has come now to examine some selected leadership styles.

## 5.3 Leadership styles

Fundamental for leadership style research are the sociological definitions regarding leadership and (especially governmental) power structures in general, as presented by Max Weber (1864-1920)[1]. For Weber, the important question was what the reasons are that lead to the legitimation of power.

---

[1]  Max, Weber, Wirtschaft und Gesellschaft, Tübingen, Mohr Siebeck, 1980

## 5.3.1 Weber

Weber distinguishes between 1) legal (rational), 2) traditional and 3) charismatic power. Legal power is based on the belief in laws as realized in a bureaucratic society. Traditional power results from the validity of structures existing from time immemorial, like for example patriarchy or feudalism. Charismatic power finally is based on the example of one individual and the order established by him.

From this, leadership style research deduced for the legal power the bureaucratic management style which focuses on guidelines, working instructions and regulations.

Traditional power is defined as paternalist management style with absolute autocracy, tight hierarchy, strict obedience and severe discipline. Charismatic power is being executed within the charismatic management style that relies on a strong personal charisma and manifests itself, according to Weber, by magic talents, revelations, heroism or by spiritual and rhetoric power.[1]

Charisma is being defined as an exceptional quality of a personality with

"superhuman...not to everybody...accessible forces or characteristics..."[2]

Robert House, American Professor for Management,[3] takes up the charismatic leadership concept by Max Weber for modern leadership style research, and he describes charismatic leaders as disposing of an unusually high dominance and self assurance as well as a striving for influence, combined with an unshakeable belief in their own values.

In his later works, House will define as criteria for charismatic leadership personalities[4],

- the criterion "assertive manner", for example assigned to personalities like John F. Kennedy or Martin Luther King, resp.

- the criterion "non-assertive manner", which he assigned to Mahatma Gandhi.

---

[1] Max Weber, Soziologie, Weltgeschichtliche Analysen, 1956

[2] Ibid., own translation

[3] Robert J. House, Theory of Charismatic Leadership, Southern Illinois University Press, 1977

[4] R. J. House, P. W. Dorfman, Cultural Influences on Organizational Leadership in: House et. al. 2004, 51

## 5.3.2 House

It is interesting that the great self-assurance of a charismatic leader is increasingly transmitting itself to the group he leads, and self-respect as well as expectations into the own performance are enhanced.

The gained performance improvement on the part of the employees, however, has to be paid with the imitation of the values of the charismatic leader. Own values and critical questioning are not developed and therefore the "magic" depends entirely on the existence of the charismatic executive. Successors of charismatic executives as well as the enterprises in question know how difficult such a situation usually is. Nevertheless, charismatic leaders are in a position to mobilize an amazing energy in their group, as they address and guide the group by emotions. House attributes the success of the charismatic leadership style also to the fact that the charismatic executive is generous with praise to his employees, that he trusts them and that with his model function he produces high credibility.

By research, however, the objection was raised[1] that trust in the employees exactly was not shown, because the charismatic executive just did not trust in own values of the employees and their own reflection.

Immanuel Kant's motto of the Age of Enlightenment was that it meant the exit from self-made mental immaturity and that mental immaturity was to be defined by the inability to make use of one's own intellect without being guided by someone else[2]. The charismatic executive, according to this, would keep his employees in this kind of mental immaturity.

Now if one would object that in the relationship with a charismatic executive, not intellect is decisive but the emotional relation to the charismatic leader, Kant's thought still remains valid. Kant does not refer to existing or not existing intellectual power but to the courage and the decision to use one's own cognitive abilities.

The claim for self-determination and critical thinking, by the way, is not systematically excluded with the exposition of charismatic leadership. It is absolutely conceivable that a charismatic executive who knows how to bind employees emotionally and to produce high moti-

---

[1] Vgl. Kuhn, 2000, Ridder, 1999
[2] Immanuel Kant, Was ist Aufklärung, Göttingen, 1994

vation and performance orientation at the same time, may demand and encourage values like autonomy and critical thinking.

After Max Weber had examined leadership within a wide sociological frame, Kurt Lewin (1890-1947)[1], a social psychologist and founder of group dynamics, introduced a fundamental economic concept of leadership style research at the end of the 1930's at the American Iowa University. Today it is often referred to as the "Iowa Studies".

### 5.3.3 Lewin

Lewin distinguishes between two management styles, 1) the autocratic management style and 2) the democratic management style. In the autocratic management style, the executive determines the working structures. Because of a dissociated personnel management, the basis for decisions as well as general targets do not become clear.

In a democratic management style, on the contrary, the executive encourages his employees to discuss the working tasks and to take part in the decisions. The executive expresses advice, praise and criticism.

In a laisser-faire management, finally, which came up as third management style rather by chance during research with youth groups of the Iowa Child Welfare Research Station, control and decision making were given completely into the hands of the group.

The authoritarian management style has the advantage of a quick reaction capacity, especially in crises, as is shown in military management. Bearing in mind McGregor's Theory X or the Rational Economic Man of Edgar Schein, the advantage here is clear responsibilities and instructions, however, on the other side, employees will not develop or maintain any initiative, especially when the executive as controlling authority is not present.

In the democratic (cooperative) management style, ideas and needs of the employees are integrated. However, here, the danger is that no clear decisions are made resp. they are made too late, and that by trying to please all people all of the time, nobody is pleased, because "Everybody's Darling is Everybody's Fool".

---

[1] Kurt Lewin, Field theory in social science (selected theoretical papers). New York, 1951

The time periods needed for decisions increase in the democratic management style and the discipline of the group of employees may deteriorate. On the other hand, a positive working climate is reached as well as the results are in favour of this management style because the performance – as was shown by the Iowa studies – remains stable, even without the executive being present. With the autocratic management style, on the contrary, the absence of the executive results in a drop of performance.

In the laisser-faire management style, employees receive a very large room for manoeuver that may be motivating, but on the other hand can also lead to a lack of discipline and orientation on the part of the employees. In the Iowa studies, the laisser-faire management happened by accident when a group, unintentionally, was left without direction. This led to bad results and even to aggressive conduct, and therefore it was deduced that any kind of management was better than none at all (or laisser-faire management).

Lewin's studies on management styles had the disadvantage that, on the one hand, the test structure with children is not quite apt to be transferred to the management situation in an enterprise and, on the other hand, that the mentioned styles of autocratic and democratic management in their polarization did not allow for a gradual continuum of ways of conduct.

At this point, the management style continuum of Robert Tannenbaum and Warren Schmidt picks up the thread. It was developed at the University of California at the end of the 1950ies.

### 5.3.4 Tannenbaum & Schmidt

Tannenbaum and Schmidt, in their executive trainings, found that executives with both management style polarities of autocratic and democratic leadership, disposed of only inadequate approaches for the variety of situations that come up in the working routine. They created a concept containing 7 styles which was supposed to offer the executives a possibility of analysis for the choice of the right management behaviour.

For this choice, executives have to adjust themselves to the variables of their own prerequisites (own skills, own values), the prerequisites of their employees (experiences, knowledge and needs) and the individual situation (company culture, company organization, task, time available).

Although the management style continuum by Tannenbaum and Schmidt continuously describes the transition between two poles, it still remains one-dimensional.

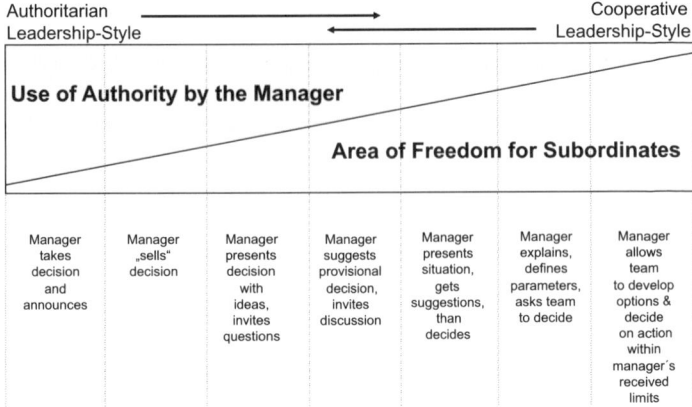

**Figure 22**  Management Style Continuum after Tannenbaum & Schmidt[1]

Hereunder, we want to look closer at the concepts of multi-dimensional management style models.

They were based on the multi-dimensional management theories of the Ohio-State University, the so-called "Ohio studies", resp. the studies of the Michigan Group[2] that were carried out at the same time.

The Ohio studies are based on a questionnaire ("Leader Behavior Description Questionnaire", LBDQ), in which employees are asked in 48 items about the behavior of their executives. The evaluation of the questionnaires showed two factors independent from each other, the employee orientation and the task orientation.

[1] R. Tannenbaum, W. H. Schmidt, How to choose a leadership pattern, Harvard Business Review 1958

[2] The definitions "Production Centered" resp. "Employee Centered" of the Michigan Studies correspond to the terms "Consideration" (Employee Centered) resp. "Initiating Structure" (Task Centered ) of the Ohio studies, see D. Tscheulin, A. Rausche, 1970. For Michigan studies see: D. Katz, N. Macoby, N. C. Morse, 1950. cp. Weibler, 2001

### 5.3.5 Gagné & Fleischmann

In the four-field matrix, the management style can now be described on both dimensions independently from each other. For example, the management behaviour of person A is characterized by a low task orientation and a middle employee orientation. Executive B, on the contrary, shows a weak employee orientation and a high orientation on the working tasks.

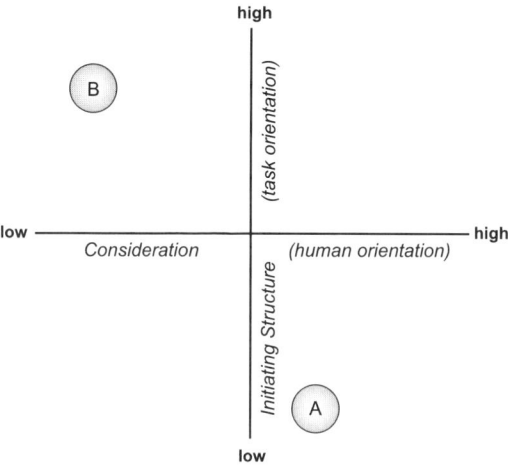

**Figure 23** C/IS-Matrix after Gagné & Fleischmann ("Ohio Studies")[1]

The Ohio studies have been criticized for the fact that both management style dimensions are not coupled with statements on contentment and performance. Employee contentment does not necessarily increase with a management style that is characterized by a high employee orientation,[2] if for instance the superior of the executive in question acts against the management style of the latter.

If one includes the variable of the organizational situation, a reciprocal proportion between employee orientation and employee contentment can even be seen when looking for example at the production area. A

---

[1] Following E. A. Fleischmann, R. M. Gagné, 1959
[2] cp. D. C. Pelz, 1952

task oriented management style may be positive in the production area, outside of it, however, it may have a negative effect.[1]

Despite of the open questions, the Ohio concept with its twofold dimensioning of task and employee orientation was subsequently in many cases taken up by management style research, for instance with the "Managerial Grid" of the American psychologist Robert Blake.

### 5.3.6 Blake & Mouton

Robert Blake (1918-2004) originally, during the 1950ies and 1960ies, worked together with Jane Mouton (1930-1987) at the Department of Psychology of the University of Texas. Later on, they both founded the Scientific Methods Inc. (later: Grid International Inc.) and in the following years, Blake taught in Harvard, Oxford and also Cambridge.

The Managerial Grid resulted from the experience that Robert Blake had gathered in the 1960's during his work with Exxon Oil Company.

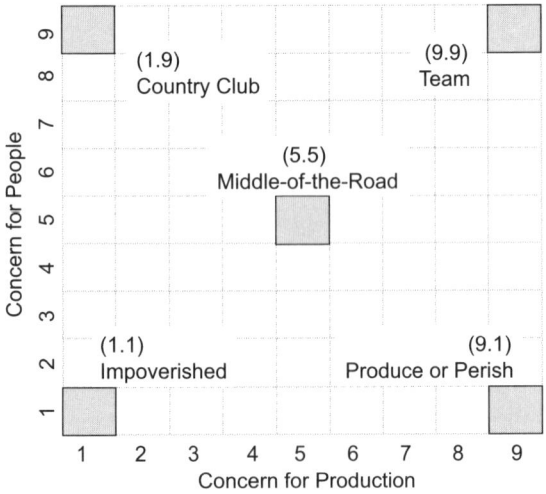

**Figure 24** Managerial Grid after Blake & Mouton[2]

[1] Fleischmann, Harris, Burtt, 1955
[2] Following Robert R. Blake, Jane S. Mouton, Verhaltenspsychologie im Betrieb, 1980

By the way, this company, in July 2008, was the company with the highest market value world wide.

Blake, together with Jane Mouton, set up the dimensions "Concern for Production" (Abscissa) and "Concern for People" (Ordinate) and divided them in 9 grades each.

Although this results in 81 possible combinations on the grid, Blake and Mouton present 5 combinations as especially typical, namely 1) Impoverished Style 2) Country-Club-Style 3) Produce or Perish-Style 4) Middle-of-the-Road Style and finally 5) Team Style. This latter "team management" is presented as the ideal management style.

As an example for the behaviour analysis with the help of the grid, 1.9 shows a "people-pleaser" who is very little interested in the technical issues of production while, on the contrary, the other extreme 9.1 describes a subject-oriented type who tries to keep out personal influence factors as much as possible, for fear that something could go wrong.

This fear can be shown in a third axis, called motivation. Thus, the third dimension of motivation from the negative extreme of motivation by fear goes to the positive extreme, motivation by desire.

We can see that the Managerial Grid, contrary to the Ohio research, is a three-dimensional model for management style research. While subject and man orientation describe the behaviour, the third dimension of motivation explains why this behaviour develops. As Robert Blake puts it himself:

> "9.1+ illustrates the desire for control and mastery – I want it to be recognized that I am in control, I tell you what to do, and you execute precisely to my requirements. I want you to recognize that you are in my hands, so that I have no question but that I've dominated the situation in which you appear. At the same corner, 9,1- represents a fear of failure. These two work together. If I need control I rely to the most limited degree possible on you, because you're liable to screw up and the failure will reflect on me. What the third dimension does is clarify the motivation underlying the grid style." [1]

Robert Blake and Jane Mouton extended the five basic styles of the managerial grid by two additional ones which are to be understood as

---

[1] Interview with Robert Blake. Healthcare Forum Journal, Vol.35, #4, 1992

combination. Thus, the so-called paternalist orientation connects fields 9.1. and 1.9. depending on the behaviour of the employee,

> "The "paternalist" style combines the whip-cracking 9.1 and the people-pleasing 1.9 depending the response of the subordinate. A subordinate that cooperates is rewarded with a "people-pleasing" relationship; one that doesn't is subjected to the whip."[1]

while the so-called "opportunist orientation" has the executive choose those combinations from all styles which are the most advantageous for himself:

> "The "opportunist," on the other hand, is a chameleon, taking on whatever grid style seems appropriate for the interaction of the moment, never revealing his or her own true feelings."[2]

When applying the managerial grid in various executive seminars, Black discovered that the self-assessment of the participants that took place before the seminar showed in 80% of the cases a 9.9 evaluation. At the end of the seminar, however, this assessment was corrected to 20%, thus corresponding to a divergence between self-image vs. outside image of 60%. Blake also compared these results on an intercultural level and, after evaluating data from more than 40 countries, found out that only percentage rates varied, not however the basic direction.

> "There is variation on that 80 percent, but the variation is a matter of degree, not a matter of direction. It is almost identical in the Soviet Union, and comparable in Britain and across Europe. In Japan, it goes from 50 percent in the pre-work to 15 percent after the seminar. These numbers have been very stable over time."[3]

The self evaluation of the executives takes place with the help of items to which correspond 6 problem fields of management, namely conflict

---

[1] Ibid.

[2] Ibid.

[3] Ibid.

resolution, taking of initiatives, information procurement, opinion building, decision taking and constructive criticism. Blake and Mouton did not give a reason why exactly these specific fields were chosen.

Robert Blake described his personal idea of man as a combination of the idealistic philosophy of Plato and the pragmatic philosophy of Aristotle. By applying both approaches, the ideal with the real, he saw the basic element for development of an executive:

> "The concept of ideal thinking came out of Plato – the "platonic ideal." Aristotle, by comparison, was the pragmatic one, the fixer, the tinkerer. It came to us suddenly that, if you put those two bases of thinking aside one another, you've got a very powerful change model. When all the people that have to live with it, and come to terms with it, do that – put the ideal in direct contrast with the real – you've got a pro-active commitment to making the change."[1]

The managerial grid by Robert Blake and Jane Mouton, successful and wide-spread, owes this not least to the fact that it was the first approach in management style research that was combined with a complete executive training. This concept, after having been many times varied and developed, is still today in operation world wide.

Like in the management style concept by Blake and Mouton which is based on the fundamental dimensions of employee orientation and task orientation from the Ohio studies, the same basis is used in another management style model by the Americans Paul Hersey (*1926) and Ken Blanchard (*1939), which has become very popular.

Moreover, the specific leadership situation which Tannenbaum and Schmidt as well as Blake and Mouton only allusively refer to, is systematically included in the model of Hersey and Blanchard. They call this third dimension the degree of maturity of the guided person and therefore the entire model is often described as "maturity model of leadership".

*"In the past a leader was a boss.*
*Today's leaders must be partners with their people.*
*They no longer can lead solely based on positional power."*
Ken Blanchard

---

[1] Ibid.

### 5.3.7 Hersey & Blanchard

Paul Hersey, behaviorist at the Nova Southeastern University, and Ken Blanchard, Professor at Cornell University, New York, are bestseller authors and successful management consultants. Blanchard is considered as one of the 10 leadership gurus of the years 2007 and 2008. The maturity model of leadership postulates that every employee should be guided in accordance to his degree of maturity, being composed of working maturity (education, knowledge, experience) and psychological maturity (performance orientation). Four grades of maturity are to be considered, Maturity M1-M4:

- *M1*
  Employees who are not willing to take over any responsibility (little psychological maturity) and who are not able to do so (little working maturity).

- *M2*
  Employees who are willing to take over responsibility (high psychological maturity), but who are not (yet) able to do so (little working maturity).

- *M3*
  Employees who are able to take over responsibility (high working maturity) but who are not willing to do so (little psychological maturity).

- *M4*
  Employees who are willing to take over responsibility (high psychological maturity) and who are able to do so (high working maturity).

Hersey and Blanchard assume in their view of the world that man during the course of his (working) life goes through a development towards increasing maturity. It is the task of the executive to find out the degree of maturity of the employee in question, in order to guide him adequate to the situation.

The level of maturity is determined by a questionnaire that measures knowledge, experience, ability to take on responsibility and willingness to perform. These characteristics are measured on a scale with eight grades and then summarized in one total. Depending on the maturity of the employee, the executive now chooses one of four management styles S1-S4:

- *S1 "Telling"*
  Exact instructions by the executive, control of performance, little relationship orientation, high task orientation.

- *S2 "Selling"*
  Directive management; intensive socio-emotional communication is supposed to lead to the acceptance of the task, high relationship orientation, high to middle task orientation.

- *S3 "Participating"*
  Active listening by the executive, common exchange of ideas leads to common decisions, executive makes task achievement easier, focus on socio-emotional support, high relationship orientation, little task orientation.

- *S4 "Delegating"*
  Executive delegates the tasks completely to the employee with occasional control, little task orientation and little relationship orientation.

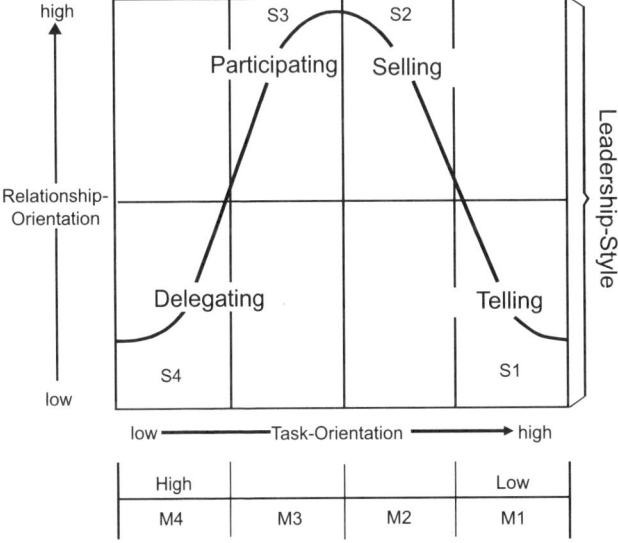

**Figure 25** Situational Leadership Theory[1]

---

[1] P. Hersey, K. Blanchard, Management of organizational behaviour: Utilizing human resources, 1987

With the situational leadership theory, after having found out from the questionnaire the degree of maturity of the employee, the executive can now, by drawing a vertical line upwards from the continuum of the degree of maturity to the point of intersection with the drawn-in graph, read the management conduct adequate to the situation.

The graph which is characteristic for the model is supposed to illustrate that the executive should not be content with limiting himself reactively to the particular level of maturity of the employee and its adequate management style, but that on the contrary he should strive to develop each employee in the direction of a maturity level as high as possible (M4 corresponding with S4). That is why the model originally was also called "Life Cycle Theory of Leadership".

Quite rightly it has been pointed out in the research literature that notwithstanding the progressive model, a congruence between the maturity level of the employee and organizational goals has been alleged.[1] As a conflict between company objective and employee objective is excluded, the concept "employee maturity" therefore may be understood ideologically.

Moreover, the model with its level of maturity only offers a situational aspect. Not only are further situational factors neglected, but also is the canon of executive behaviour limited to the four management styles S1-S4. The infinite variety of individual employee characteristics therefore necessarily has to be reduced to these existing categories.

After having gone from management with its underlying different ideas of man to the presentation of some selected management styles, we now want to discuss some typical additional management techniques. These management techniques describe in addition to the categorization of styles concrete behavior patterns in their application.

## 5.4 Management Techniques

The most widely used management technique probably is Management by Objectives (MbO). Less common are Management by Delegation

---

[1] Neuberger, 1995

(MbD) or Managment by Exception (MbE). The list of such definitions may of course be extended as far as one likes. [1]

## 5.4.1 Management by Delegation

Management by Delegation (MbD) which is based on the sixth, cooperative management style in the continuum of Tannenbaum and Schmidt, wants on the one hand to relieve executives from the quantity of decisions, and on the other hand, by delegation of tasks, it intends to strengthen initiative, willingness to take over responsibility and performance orientation on the part of the employees.

This requires that tasks are being transferred including competences and room for manoeuvre. However, by procuring at the same time the corresponding working instructions and process descriptions (rules for exceptions, information, control system, reporting system, performance indicators, etc.), the employee is to be offered sufficient structural tools in order to be able to meet these responsibilities.

A condition for the readiness to delegation on the part of the executives is that they trust their employees and that the employees, in their turn, are in a position to deal with the delegation appropriately as regards ability and willingness. The strongly task-oriented view of the Management by Delegation may possibly neglect process aspects, general objective orientation or even motivation aspects, for example in cases where only those tasks would be delegated that are annoying to the executive.

In its generality, Management by Delegation scarcely goes beyond the delegative management style as far as concrete acting instructions are concerned and thus remains as management technique relatively vague.

## 5.4.2 Management by Exception

Management by Exception (MbE) views management on the aspect of exception and divergence. In a way comparable to the laisser-faire management, MbE leaves employees to their work until a divergence or a

---

[1] Hentze/Brose, for example, distinguish 8 subject oriented and 7 individual oriented "Management-by" approaches, 1986

problem that cannot be solved makes necessary the intervention of the executive. Up to the point where a problem has to be solved, this management technique, like that of MbD, has as condition a strongly formalized and detailed framework of rules, in which also the exceptional case calling for redelegation to the executive is precisely described in the course of the process.

The one-sided, incomplete focus on the divergence from the authorized process does not really give clarity to the employees as regards target strategy and therefore does not enhance initiative or motivation. Also the learning process of the employees in the insoluble exceptional case has to be ensured for their development's sake, and it also has to be avoided that an executive would establish himself in the role of the "rescuer" on a permanent basis.

### 5.4.3 Management by Objectives

With Management by Objectives (MbO), target agreements between executive and employee are made which correspond to clearly formulated targets (at best as defined by S.M.A.R.T, see Chapter 2.3.1). This management technique is supposed to increase the transparency of the target achievement, thus also increasing the quality of the working performance as well as the motivation of the employees, as for example the compensation of the employees may be tied to the attainment of goals which have been agreed upon.

This requires within the organization of an enterprise an institutionalized, regularly repeated performance management process as well as a controlling system for quality assurance. MbO together with a controlling instrument like the balanced score card, for example, represents a very powerful combination for the agreement and follow-up of targets.

The targets of a department, of a group and of every individual employee are deduced from the overall company targets resp. from the company strategy. Level by level, they are then broken down in a top-down process, and then the individual target fulfilment or possibly a new definition of the overall targets or strategies is being reported back in a bottom-up feedback process.

Despite of the fact that Management by Objectives with all its advantages is widely used, it should not be ignored that for example regarding target pooling (interdependent target conflicts and dependencies of particular areas and departments) or especially globalized strategies, the

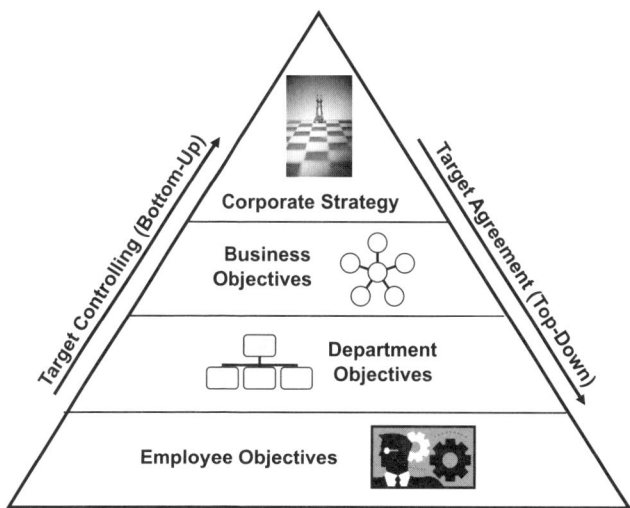

**Figure 26** Process of Target Agreement and Feedback

MbO strategy has to be adapted to particular needs when, for instance, individual MbO definitions focusing on the occident have to be transformed to targets for groups situated in collectivistic oriented cultures. It therefore makes sense to put our attention in the following to some essential facts to be observed when Leadership takes place on an international level.

# Intercultural Leadership – HR Management in a Globalized World Economy

> *"He who knows himself and others*
> *Here will also see,*
> *That the East and West, like brothers,*
> *Parted ne'er shall be.*
> *Thoughtfully to float for ever*
> *'Tween two worlds, be man's endeavor!*
> *So between the East and West*
> *To revolve, be my behest!"*
>
> Johann Wolfgang Goethe (1749-1832),
> West-Eastern Divan

Light-hearted and carefree – this is how Goethe anticipates globalization, but hard is the path when looking from the anthropological whole to the cultural speciality and when we examine concrete fields of action that make international management so complex. Why Japanese employees cannot be directed like American ones following the Management by Objectives principles? What difference is there between commitment and motivation resp. rejection shown in the European and the Asian part of the world? What rules have to be observed regarding punctuality for meetings and negotiations, and why is it that two countries geographically side by side may differ in their company hierarchies much more than others situated far away from each other?

Many popular examples for different behaviour can be found. For instance we find it normal in the Western world to keep eye contact while in some Islamic countries this may be improper between men and women. In India, shaking of the head in fact means "yes", while Asians will avoid to give a "no" as reply from fear to make the addressee lose face. They will rather stay evasive.

In Asia, it is advantageous to get in contact with business partners with the help of an older person disposing of a certain status because this

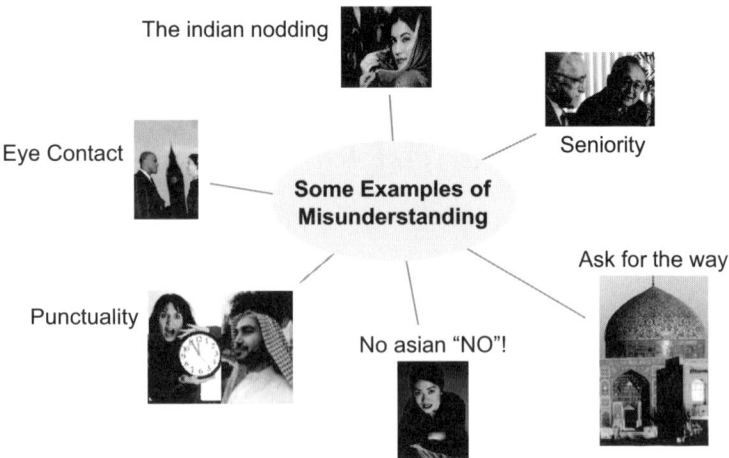

**Figure 27** Examples of Cultural Misunderstandings

status may then be transferred to oneself. When asking someone the way in Iran, one will most probably get an affirmative answer in any case, even if the way is not known, because here the focus is on the social obligation to be of help. Also, dealing with time will for instance be very different in South American or Arab countries when compared with our absolute punctuality here in Europe. Many more examples could be cited.

For medium-sized companies doing business on an international level as well as for multinational companies, it is essential to dispose of an extensive arsenal of management techniques to help them survive in a globalized economy. Over a long time the conviction has been growing that management methods that were successful at home could possibly not be applied globally without limitations. This conviction, unfortunately, is still not paid enough attention to when it comes to practical consequences, especially regarding leadership, communication or decision processes.

Still, many internationally active enterprises have meanwhile started, when filling jobs at foreign branch offices, to increasingly hire local managers, instead of the usual method by which managers from the headquarter are delegated to "do missionary work" at the foreign subsidiaries.

A certain cultural change is also happening because of the increasing use of modern media. Especially in times of tight budgets, telephone and video conferences can efficiently save travelling costs and time resources. With this change of mind and habit also came along different needs concerning the assignment of responsibilities in the mother companies.

To the same extent as times have changed when only a small number of foreign delegates had to know all about intercultural habits and nowadays also hierarchies especially in the Western enterprises tend to become more and more flat, a great many employees in international companies see themselves confronted with the necessity to deal with intercultural responsibilities in their working routine. To begin with, a distinction has to be made between the different levels that are crossed by the organizational culture of an internationally active enterprise, resp. attention has to be paid to how this organizational culture itself is set up.

## 6.1 Organizational Cultures

Edgar Schein, whom we have already met in the last chapter, distinguishes the organizational culture on three successively following levels, 1) the basic assumptions, 2) the values situated on top of them, and finally 3) the expressed artefacts.

Although the artefacts are very well perceptible, their classification remains polyvalent, the reason of which may be their symbolic character. Underneath this visible phenomenal level are situated the collective values, already describing concrete behavioural standards and their assessment.

Schein here distinguishes once more between assumed virtual values – which may be deducted from company principles or guidelines, but often remain a wish and a theoretical ideal – and internalized values that concretely have manifested themselves in the behavior. Finally, in the basic assumptions, all those values are embodied that have become part of the disposition of an enterprise or their members and are not questioned any more.

Even if these value assumptions have a most important influence on behavior, they are at work secretly and it is difficult to make them transparent. Schein establishes a correlation between the functionality of the different cultural levels and elements and the efficiency of enterprises, attaching a special importance to the basic assumptions.

To be able to realize an organizational culture necessitates an observer who besides his professionalism also disposes of "visitor's eyes", which means that he should not be member of this culture himself.

An organizational culture is not built up in a monolithic way but is fragmented again, depending on qualities and quantities of an enterprise, in many horizontal and vertical subcultures that exist side by side and may work together cooperatively but also against each other, as can often be seen, especially after a merger.

With reference to an international environment, when adding the specific regional culture in which an enterprise is embedded, we are dealing with a variety of cultures that all interact and are related to each other.

If one relates this view on subcultures to human resources management or the personnel management strategy of an international enterprise, we will see that one cannot really talk of "the" human resources strategy of an enterprise unless it is bundled up in an international strategy.

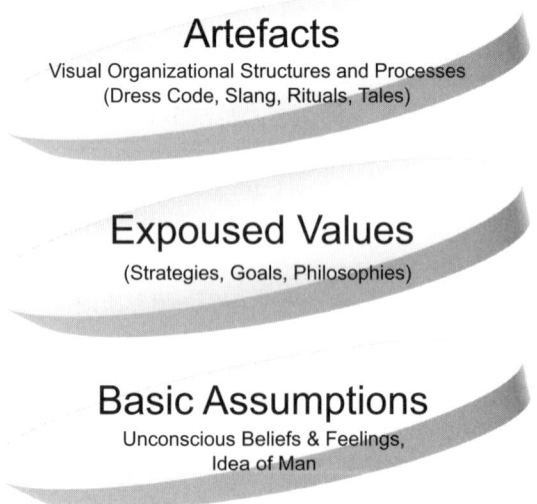

**Figure 28** Three Levels of Organizational Culture after Edgar Schein[1]

---

[1] Edgar H. Schein, Organizational Culture and Leadership, 2003

Chapter 6: Intercultural Leadership

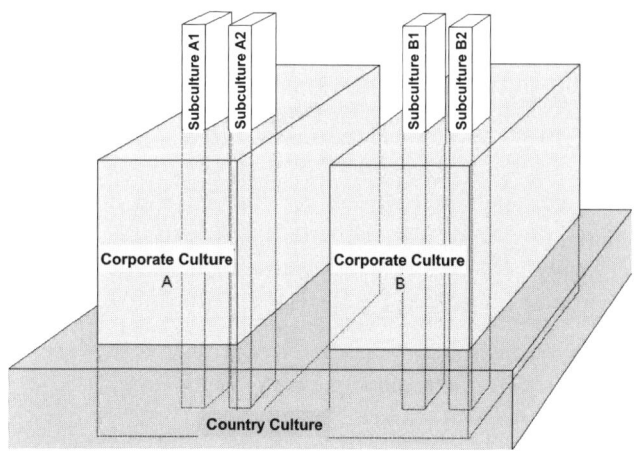

Labels within figure:
Subculture A1, Subculture A2, Subculture B1, Subculture B2, Corporate Culture A, Corporate Culture B, Country Culture

**Figure 29** Organizational Subcultures[1]

While on the one hand, on the level of the purely operational person-nel work, already for practical reasons – if we think for example only of the varying labour law in the different countries – a central human re-sources management frequently is not successful, on the other hand the necessity for it is often neglected when it comes to the strategic, con-ceptual personnel work. Theory distinguishes three archetypal strate-gies as regards cultures, 1) monocultural, 2) multicultural and 3) mixed-culture strategies.

## 6.2 Culture Strategies, Decision Finding and Internationalization

While the monocultural strategy means that the culture of the mother company is simply transferred to the subsidiaries, the multicultural strategy leaves to each subsidiary its own heterogeneous structure. A mixed-culture strategy tries to mix elements of mother company and subsidiaries, thereby corresponding to the idea of interdependent learning from each other with the objective of enriching the predomi-nant culture by the others.

---

[1] Following C. Scholz, 2000, modified

Monocultural strategies contain implicitly a value judgment, assuming that the own company culture is to be seen superior to the foreign one. In the extreme, this could end up in cultural imperialism where own values are transferred and local company culture is completely ignored and suppressed.

The liberality of the multicultural strategy theoretically leaves untouched the variety in values of the different subsidiaries. In practice, however, one would expect that at least the basic elements of the company philosophy will be transferred to the foreign branch.

The mixed-culture strategy finally represents the only case where a feedback takes place from the headquarter to the subsidiaries.

After having taken notice of what kind of cultural strategy is applied, we do not dispose yet of any information on the question how decisions are made in an enterprise – centralized in the headquarter, decentralized in the different subsidiaries, or federally in a common integrated system. When combining cultural and decision finding strategies in an enterprise, nine strategies of internationalization can be distinguished.

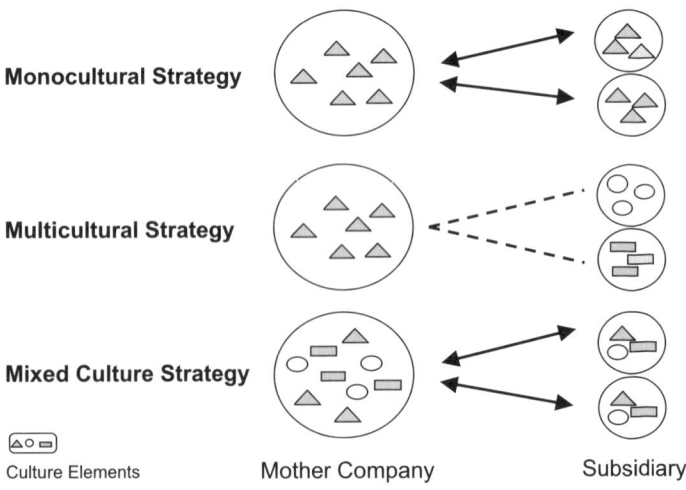

**Figure 30** Cultural Strategies[1]

---

[1] Following C. Scholz, 2000, modified

| Culture Strategy / Decision-finding Strategies | Monocultural Strategy | Multicultural Strategy | Mixed Culture Strategy |
|---|---|---|---|
| central | (1) | (2) | (3) |
| decentral | (4) | (5) | (6) |
| federal | (7) | (8) | (9) |

**Figure 31** Strategies of Internationalization[1]

Field (1) describes a transfer of the organizational culture into the subsidiaries; all decisions are made centrally. Despite of the central decision-making authority by the mother company, in field (2) cultural differences of the subsidiaries are tolerated and in certain cases even welcomed, for instance, if they may be used for a production advantage. Field (3), despite of a direct central decision-making authority, could lead in the long term to an intercultural mixture even up to the upper management levels at the headquarters, and the question suggests itself if this does not weaken the central decision-making authority.

Variation (4) describes many "royal courts" as regards to decision-making authority, however, all subsidiaries remain tied together by a basic culture. Fields (5) and (8) represent in their combination of decentralized resp. federal decision-making and multicultural strategies the highest possible diversification of all nine strategies of internationalization.

Fields (6) and (9) tolerate, despite a liberal decision-making strategy, the mixture of local societal cultures, which theoretically may in the longer run develop into a synergetic culture for all countries. The difference to fields (5) and (8), however, only lies in the particular mixing ratio of the

---

[1] Ibid.

portions of local culture, and therefore the development of a relatively stable mixed culture with a similar monolithic effect as a new monoculture is practically rather improbable. If, despite of federal decision-making structures, a homogeneous organizational culture should nevertheless establish itself, this might possibly be due to its growing attractiveness (field 7).

Neither are these new strategies of internationalization in theory easily to be clearly rated, nor can they in practice be divided properly. Central strategies will always have a tendency to bring about the advantage of standardization, empirical experience and therefore quality assurance. On the other hand, in their stability and rigidity they will not be able to react quickly and flexibly to market situations, and they will neither look for new innovative solutions nor will they value them, let alone integrate them into the own system.

Also, a monocultural organizational strategy may be beneficial to employee identity, to the sense of being part of a community as well as to motivation. On the other hand, multicultural and mixed culture strategies will rather be more suitable in practice if the intention is to leave existing societal identities and take advantage of the particular local competition opportunities. This strategy may be especially efficient when looking for international production locations.

After having examined basic strategies of internationalization, we should now think about a coherent strategy for human resources. In the cases where delegation is the preferred strategy, we can distinguish three prototypes: 1) Country Manager, 2) Global Manager, and 3) Company Manager.[1]

A Country Manager is an expert for certain societal cultures who has been specifically trained for this demand. The culture specific basis can be obtained not only from experiences of formerly delegated employees who may prepare seminars, but also from meanwhile numerous and comprehensive studies that deduce cultural characteristics from empirical studies.

A Global Manager is not limited to specific countries and cultural contexts. He is, on the contrary, a generalist who probably corresponds best to the common ideal of an international executive. He is able to adjust himself flexibly to the prevailing cultural circumstances.

---

[1]  C. Scholz, 2000

The Company Manager, finally, represents deliberately his own company and societal culture. His assignment can usefully be combined with a monocultural strategy. A Country Manager is best adapted to a multicultural strategy, while the Global Manager will best work in a mixed culture strategy.

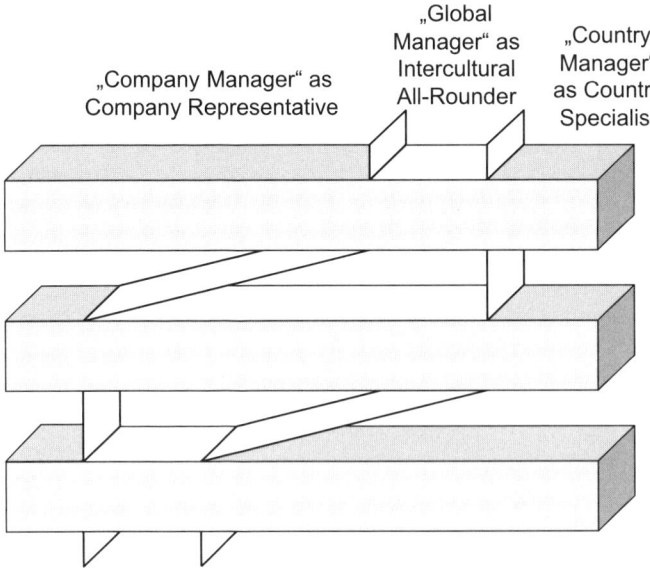

**Figure 32** Guidelines for International Managers[1]

We now come to the delegation of a so-called "Expatriate Manager" to the foreign division for a certain time (mostly we distinguish between a short-term delegation – up to one year – and a long-term delegation – up to three or more years). When selecting the training as a preparation for the stay abroad, one will have to keep in mind not only the length of the stay, but also how much time for the preparation is available and what organizational cultures are involved.

Intercultural trainings, moreover, have to take into consideration the particular target group, their interests and levels of hierarchy and, of

---

[1]  C. Scholz, 2000, modified

course, the purpose of the planned assignment. Basic information on the host country can easily be obtained from books, films or lectures by former expatriates returned home. Additionally, for the transition from a purely cognitive comprehension of facts to the deepening of felt contents, methods are available which relate the values of the own culture to that of the foreign culture, make them transparent and – by means of case analyses, role plays and simulations – bring about trained behaviour modifications.

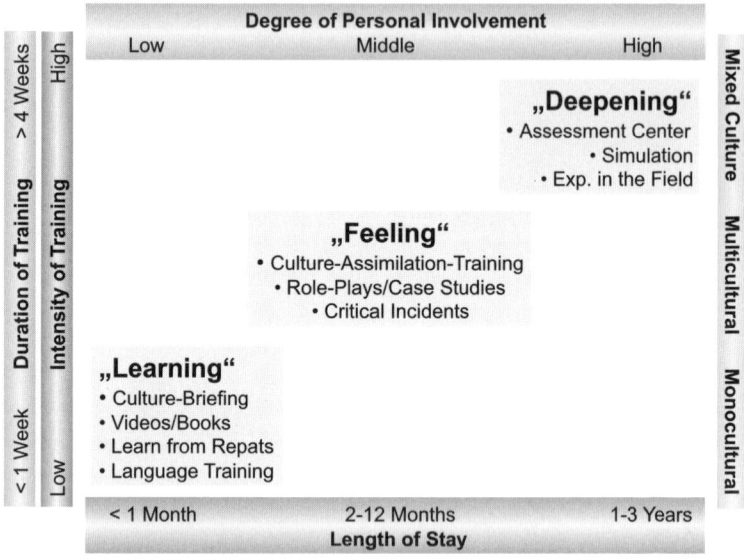

**Figure 33** Decision Finding for Intercultural Training[1]

Mendenhall, Dunbar & Oddou claim in their model a correlation between the necessary acculturation level and the integration level, because a short stay in a foreign subsidiary situated in an area which differs strongly from one's own company and societal culture might possibly require a bigger effort of acculturation than a longer stay in a nearly related cultural environment.

---

[1] Model for the Selection of Training Measures as Preparation for a Stay Abroad, modified after M. E. Mendenhall, E. Dunbar, G. R. Oddou, Expatriate Selection, Training and Career Pathing. A Review and Critique, in HRM 26, 1987, 331-345

We are now at a point where the frequently used term "culture" should be defined somewhat clearer.

## 6.3 Cultural Dimensions and Expressions

The American anthropologist Clyde Kluckhohn (1905-1960) described man "in a certain aspect like all, some and no other man".[1] What he wanted to say is that culture cannot be understood as basic and common human nature shared by all human beings, nor as personality description of an individual with unique occurence.

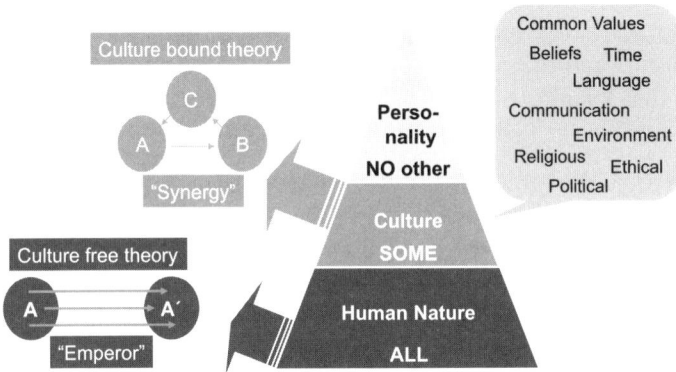

**Figure 34** Anthropology and Culture

The Dutchman Geert Hofstede, Professor Emeritus of the University of Maastricht, describes culture as something that we share with some other people regarding common values, language, religion or political convictions.

*"Culture is the collective programming of the mind*
*which distinguishes one group of people from another."* [2]

*Geert Hofstede*

---

[1]  C. Kluckhohn, H. A. Murray, Personality in Nature, Culture and Society, 1948. Cp. G. Hofstede, 2006, 4

[2]  G. Hofstede, 1984

## 6.3.1 Hofstede (*1928)

With the work of Hofstede, a notion of culture established itself that, in intercultural research as well as in fundamental paradigms which are part of intercultural trainings, has shifted the centre of gravity from a culture-free theory to a culture-bound theory.

While the culture-free theory sees man anthropologically as essentially equal and often puts a focus on phylogenetic transmission – therefore treating specific cultural factors as negligible – the culture-bound theory, on the contrary, claims the perception and application of cultural characteristics as special factor of success for intercultural management, for instance with regards to organization, personnel and negotiation management.

Actual research (GLOBE Study of 62 Societies, 2004[1]) supports the culture-bound theory. When connoting the culture-bound theory with societal culture and the culture-free theory with business culture, it can be seen that for successful management the socio-cultural influence is to be rated 10 times higher than the business one.[2]

In a value-related consideration, the culture-free theory may be compared to a universalism which, when for example occurring as western cultural imperialism, does not acknowledge traditions and values of other countries. Certain values with a universalistic claim like human rights, democracy or equal rights may therefore possibly break against particular societal cultures.

A culture-bound theory, on the contrary, corresponds to a value relativism which in the sense of a multicultural strategy acknowledges and tolerates foreign cultures, resp. in the sense of a mixed-culture strategy even assimilates these elements in a synergetic way.

Geert Hofstede, as representative of the culture-bound theory, was the first (1967-1973) to do a research by means of an empirical study with 117,000 IBM employees in 67 countries on basic cultural differences. He summarized and defined five cultural dimensions, namely 1) individualism vs. collectivism (IDV), 2) masculinity vs. femininity (MAS), 3) power distance index (PDI), 4) uncertainty avoidance index (UAI) and finally 5) long-term orientation vs. short-term orientation (LTO).

---

[1] P. W. Dorfman, R. House, Cultural Influences on Organizational Leadership, in: House, 2004, 53

[2] Cp. F. C. Brodbeck et al., 2002 and 2008

To begin with, let us examine the meanings assigned to these terms by Geert Hofstede.

## Individualism

Frank Sinatra's song "I did it my way" very well expresses the American need for independence, liberty and individualism, and therefore no-one will be amazed if in the cultural dimensions index, America reaches world wide the highest values as regards individualism. This means high working mobility, high self-centeredness and a preference for individual decisions. Hofstede was able to make out a positive correlation between the prosperity of a country and its individualism score. According to that, poorer countries are clearly less individualistically oriented than richer ones.

## Collectivism

Over many years, at Shinjuku Station in Tokyo (biggest train station in the world) one could read signs with the request to please not commit suicide on the rails during rush hours. What in a Western, individualistic culture will produce incomprehension may remain very valid as sense of community in a strongly collectivistic culture like Japan, even in extreme conflict and emergency situations.

Collective orientation may mean for instance in working life to see the own enterprise as family that one would not leave at the first given opportunity, even if the conditions offered somewhere else were better. Management by Objectives has to orientate itself on team targets; personal competition between employees ("Employee of the Month") cannot just be taken over from an individualistic culture. In collectivistic societies it is rather probable that sons will professionally follow in their fathers' footsteps than in individualistic societies.[1]

## Masculinity

Values like self-assertiveness, ambition, material success or individual performance orientation in competition to others are defined by Hofstede as masculine values.

---

[1] Cp. G. Hofstede, 2006, 133

Quicker – higher – further are masculine cultural values that Hofstede assigns rather to countries in equator proximity or with a Catholic population, contrary to Protestant countries. Romanic countries like France or Belgium and also Nordic countries like Denmark, Norway or Sweden have a lower masculinity score than for instance Anglo-American or German speaking countries. Also typical for a masculine culture is the decreasing separation between high career orientation and private life. Work and leisure time are hardly separated any more.

*Femininity*

A feminine approach would allow for a work-life balance which by renunciation of competition, stress and high life speed attaches greater importance to inner harmony as well as balance between professional demands and family resp. general life quality. In the working environment, this will come along with a more agreeable relationship between the levels of hierarchy, professional security and a focus on social contacts. While, in a masculine society, the working morale would be: "Live in order to work", in a feminine society it would rather read: "Work in order to live."[1]

*Power Distance*

Strong power distance in a culture is reflected by a strong company hierarchy and here also, Hofstede was able to show a positive correlation of power distance tolerance for Southern countries as well as population density, and a negative correlation to the prosperity of a country. However, here too Belgium and France are an exception. Accordingly, flat hierarchies and flexible organizational and project structures become possible in organizational cultures with low power distance scores.

*Uncertainty Avoidance*

Uncertainty avoidance as anthropological constant factor of human life is being found everywhere, however, the degree of an accepted basic anxiety that evolutionarily comes walking along with uncertainty is strongly varying, especially depending on the political history of a country. Thus, young democracies like Germany or Austria show stron-

---

[1]  G. Hofstede, 2006, 197

ger uncertainty avoiding tendencies than more established ones like England or the USA. In an enterprise, a tendency to uncertainty avoidance normally will lead to a strong structure and a high degree of standardization. A high uncertainty avoidance score will have the management focus on operational work, while strategic management would require as prerequisite to be prepared to take risks.[1]

## Short-Term Orientation

Short-term orientation focuses on profit and result and accordingly applies to presence or past and refers to tradition. Short-term orientation will be found in most of the European countries as well as in the USA and it rather acknowledges strong individuals, prompt satisfaction of demands and consumerism with competition and trend elements (products in fashion, keeping up with the social milieu).

## Long-Term Orientation

Long-term orientation is characterized by long-term company targets and also long-term profit expectations. Accordingly, qualities like being economical, persevering and persistent are acknowledged, as well as subordination under given purposes and objectives. The focus is the fu-

| Country | IND | MAS | UAI | PDI | LTO |
|---|---|---|---|---|---|
| Australia | 90 | 61 | 51 | 36 | 31 |
| Germany | 67 | 66 | 65 | 35 | 31 |
| France | 71 | 43 | 86 | 68 | - |
| Italy | 76 | 70 | 75 | 50 | - |
| Japan | 46 | 95 | 92 | 54 | 80 |
| Netherlands | 80 | 14 | 53 | 38 | 44 |
| Austria | 55 | 79 | 70 | 11 | - |
| Sweden | 71 | 5 | 29 | 31 | 33 |
| Switzerland | 68 | 70 | 58 | 34 | - |
| South Africa | 65 | 63 | 49 | 49 | - |
| USA | 91 | 62 | 46 | 40 | 29 |

**Figure 35** Comparison of Culture Scores of Selected Countries (IND = Individualism, MAS = Masculinity, UAI = Uncertainty Avoidance, PDI = Power Distance, LTO = Long-term Orientation)

---

[1] G. Hofstede, 2006, 255

ture. As these are values coming especially from the Confucian philosophy, this dimension has been called "Confucian Working Dynamics"[1] which today plays a role in most different Asian cultures like China, Japan or South Korea.

In figure 35 a list of selected countries is presented giving an overall view of the scores reached in the study by Geert Hofstede:

The statements contained in Hofstede's culture scores may be directly used in management. For example, they help answer the question if and in how far a management technique like MbO should be applied in individualistic cultures in the form of individual target agreements. Obviously, with increasing collectivism, it will make sense to make more and more group target agreements.

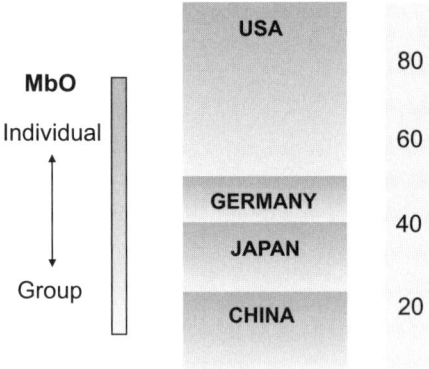

**Figure 36** Dimension Scores for Individualism

Again, referring to suitable management styles, those with an authoritarian tendency may be rather expected to be gradually found in countries with a high power-distance score, resp. a participatory or cooperative management style will be rather found in organizational cultures with low hierarchies.

Hofstede has shown in his comparison of index scores that regionally close countries, as far as culture dimensions are concerned, are not always more similar to one another than regionally distant ones. For ex-

---

[1] G. Hofstede (after Michael Bond), 2006, 292

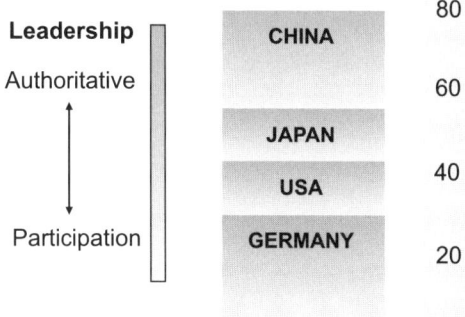

| Leadership | CHINA | 80 |
| Authoritative | | 60 |
| | JAPAN | |
| | USA | 40 |
| Participation | GERMANY | 20 |

**Figure 37** Dimension Scores for Power Distance

ample, Germany in its prevailing hierarchical structure, is nearer to the USA than to its European neighbour France where strong power distance characteristics can be found.

Although France as well as Austria both show strong individuality scores, in Austria this correlates with a culture of little power distance while France shows a high power-distance score. Hofstede therefore calls Frenchmen "dependent individualists".

The fit of different cultures, especially organizational culture vs. societal culture, may very well be visualized by means of radar charts. Thereby, an enterprise is able to anticipate, before doing another step further in internationalization, where the societal culture corridor is violated and therefore, with high probability, difficulties are to be expected.

When visualizing the culture chart, we can see potential conflicts between the French mother and the Danish subsidiary. An executive sent from France to Denmark will most probably, because of the existing PDI delta, with his authoritarian management style upset Danish employees who are used to a participatory and cooperative management. Moreover, because of the UAI delta, he may possibly attract attention with his tendency to standardised bureaucratic rules and standards. If an executive does not have the chance to learn about such cultural differences in advance, he may be doomed to fail because of the impression he possibly gives the Danes as "authoritarian bureaucrat, afraid to make decisions".

The studies by Hofstede were the first comprehensive approach in intercultural research alone for the mere quantity of empirical data. The

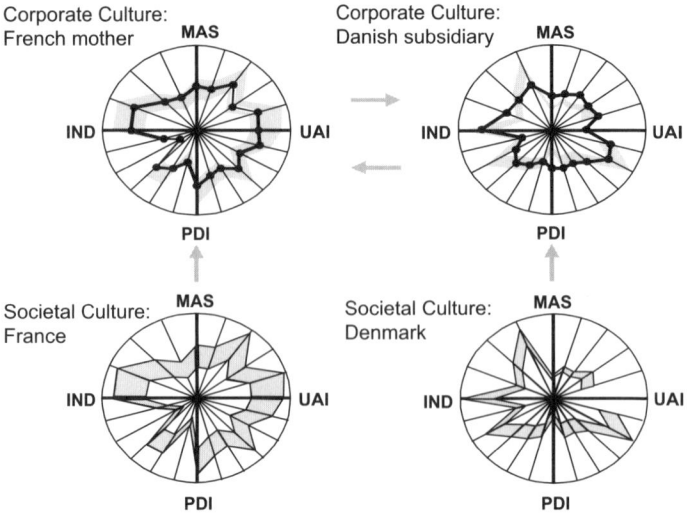

**Figure 38** Culture Charting[1]

question arises, however, if the presented number of five cultural dimensions is sufficient – a question, though, that Hofstede asked himself as well.

The study was made at the end of the 1960s and in the meantime has lost some of its relevance. The limitation to the organizational culture of IBM and therefore the restriction to one industrial sector and only a certain section of interviewed persons have been subject to criticism by intercultural research over the years, as well as the fact that the interview questions were oriented on a Western culture only.

As a whole, however, not only the basic statements of Hofstede have proven to be relatively appropriate but they also correlated with other independent studies that were made later on.

Until today, Hofstede's cultural concept again and again was subject to extensions and supplementations. For instance, one dimension that Hofstede had not taken into consideration is the comprehension of and dealing with time. This time dimension, however, was closely examined by Robert Levine, American scientist and professor for psychology

---

[1]  C. Scholz, 2000, 843, modified

at the California State University, who – among other things – compared the walking speed in different parts of the world in order to deduce therefrom the cultural speed of life.

## 6.3.2 Robert Levine (*1945)

The observation of a correlation between individualism and higher prosperity confirmed by Hofstede and later on by Trompenaars, was enlarged additionally by Robert Levine with the discovery of an increased living speed.[1] His statement was that individualistic thinking enhanced time pressure which, in its turn, favoured a productive economy and this again, in the medium-term, would increase the standard of living and contentment.

Therefore, on the whole, he assumes that man in an individualistic culture with higher living speed is happier. Individualistic cultures would attach more importance to performance than to team spirit.[2] Also, the view that love should precede marriage would distinguish individualistic from collectivistic cultures.[3]

In the meantime, doubts have come up in research about the stated connection between individualism and prosperity and also about the question if one is caused by the other or vice versa. Bhawuk, Bechthold and Munusami, on the contrary, even postulate a correlation between collectivism and national prosperity. At the actual point of research we have to assume that no clear correlation between individualism resp. collectivism and economic prosperity can be observed.[4]

Levine, interestingly enough, even notes a relation between an inner sense of time and the outdoor temperature, meaning that people that live in warmer regions also live with a slower running inner clock. Analogically, high fever would give us the impression that time is passing

---

[1]  R. Levine, 1992

[2]  R. Levine, 1997, 211

[3]  R. Levine, 1995, 554-571

[4]  Cp. D. P. S. Bhawuk, D. J. Bechthold, V. Munusami, Culture and economic Success: Is individualism the only way?, 2003, ibid. S. H. Schwartz, Beyond Individualism and Collectivism; New cultural dimensions of values, in: Kim/Traindis/Kagitcibasi/Choi/Yoon (Eds.) Individualism and collectivism: Theory, method and applications, 85-122, Newbury Park, CA, Sage, 1994, cp. also M.Gelfand, D. P. S. Bhawuk, L. H. Nishii, D. J.Bechthold, Individualism and Collectivism, House, 2004, 437

slower than it really does.[1] Also, so he says, could it be shown that processes taking place in the right half of the brain like music, painting, emotion were difficult to assess as to their length of time.

In reminiscence of the flow concept of the American professor of psychology Mihaly Csikzentmihalyi, it would be characteristic in this state of consciousness when being totally absorbed by the actually executed activity, that time had no sensible qualitative equivalent any more for the flow experience. In other words, in the state of contemplation, concentration and complete absorption in the NOW, in the flow the feeling for time would get lost.

According to Levine, independent of the also existing individual genetic dispositions for time perception, in the cultural macrocosm of the Arabic world one could make out only three time states, "no time", "now" and "eternal". Thus, the misunderstandings with Western cultures when fixing business appointments could easily be explained. An Arab being half an hour late according to Western time, would have an individual feeling of being perhaps only 10 minutes late. One should wait at least 30 minutes or longer for him, otherwise HE would feel hurt.[2]

In Japan, for instance, it would be important to be quick at work, this also meaning to move quickly, regardless if required or not. Although the working burden was high, the Japanese would not feel the pressure, among others due to the fact that the working day was long but not exclusively adjusted to productivity. For example, working colleagues usually also belonged to the circle of friends.

And – also contrary to the Western world – the Japanese would believe that what they desired would be rather realized if they kept back, while in the Western world an active request and the explicit saying would be part of the individual idea of performance. This point of view resembles the statement of Fons Trompenaars with his contrasting pair of performance vs. background (see below).

In countries like Brazil or Iran, feelings of people and the social obligation were more important than correct information transfer. Thus, people would offer information or make promises even without disposing of the corresponding knowledge or power, just in order not to loose their face.

---

[1]  Ibid., 60
[2]  R. Levine, 1997, 253

The American anthropologist Edward Hall – at about the same time as Geert Hofstede's studies took place, at the end of the 1960s – distinguished, when talking about the dealing with time in different cultures, between the polarities "monochronous" ("time is money") and "polychronous" ("jam karet" = Balinese: "elastic time").

### 6.3.3  Edward Hall (*1914)

Hall distinguishes between monochronous cultures – appreciating punctuality, time scheduling and linearity – and polychronous cultures dealing flexibly with time resp. subordinate time to human relations. Polychronous cultures would not assume linear, gradual processes but parallel and simultaneous ones. Accordingly, tasks would not necessarily be worked off step-by-step, but the working processes would flow into each other; time would be "juggled" with.

This understanding of time might well have an influence on the working and living rhythm. Accordingly, monochronous, Western, individualistic cultures would tend towards dynamic movements, big steps, moving arms[1], while polychronous cultures would express themselves rather by a slow and flowing body language. These characteristics would have to be seen in connection with the specific regional living speed.

Additionally, Hall establishes a concordance of polychronous and context-dependent cultural understanding. Concerning communication, which is his point of comparison between the cultures, he distinguishes context-bound and context-independent cultures.

Rather context-bound cultures, among which Hall counts the Arab nations, China, Japan, Korea or the Mediterranean area, would use to a high degree non-verbal communication, i. e. facial play, gestures and body language.

Rather context-independent cultures like USA, Germany or Switzerland would focus on the contents of the communication, and accordingly communication there would be explicit, direct and unambiguous, therefore typical for individualistic cultures. "Yes" meant "yes", and "no" meant "no".

---

[1]  Cp. S. Molcho, 1988, 178

Besides Hofstede, Levine and Hall we would also like to shortly mention the intercultural research of Fons Trompenaars, a disciple of Geert Hofstede.

### 6.3.4 Fons Trompenaars (*1952)

Trompenaars' research is, like that of Hofstede, supported by an empirical study with interviews of 46,000 managers from different companies in 50 countries in the 1980s and 1990s. Trompenaars found out seven contrast dimensions, 1) universalism vs. particularism, 2) neutrality vs. emotionality, 3) individualism vs. collectivism, 4) specificity vs. diffusiveness, 5) achievement vs. ascription, 6) way of dealing with the environment, and finally 7) way of dealing with time.[1] Trompenaars, contrary to Hofstede, does not indicate total scores for the different dimensions.

*1) Universalism vs. Particularism*
describes the general radius, effect and validity of regulations within a society, while "particularism" tolerates specific situations and individual exceptions of the prevailing legalities. With a universalistic culture probably comes along a higher degree of standardization, as for example in U.S. American enterprises. Particularistic cultures will put a stronger focus on personal relations than on abstract regulations. This can be observed for instance when doing business with Asian countries.

*2) Neutrality vs. Emotionality*
Neutrality describes a low degree of expressed feelings or also a lower degree of expressed gestures, facial play as well as a moderate speaking voice. Compared to this kind of cultural expression that seems to be more disciplined, "emotionality" gives the impression of impulsiveness and of rather referring to human relations than to facts.

*3) Individualism vs. Collectivism*
The differentiation between "individualism" and "collectivism" essentially follows that of Hofstede. The correlation there between individualism and economic success is reflected in Trompenaars' correlative of market-economy oriented countries and individualism.

*4) Specificity vs. Diffusiveness*
Similarly, when coming to the contrasting pair "specificity vs. diffusiveness", emotional control and a clear and functional language is meant

---

[1] Trompenaars, Riding the Waves of Culture, 1993

whenever a culture is characterized as "specific", while passionate and ornate expressions would describe a "diffusive" culture. "Specificity" additionally concerns a high degree of separation between private, inner areas and more outside ones. This kind of separation, for instance, is made to a far lesser degree by Asians with their tendency to "diffusiveness" than by Americans, Canadians or Swiss people.

"Specific" cultures, for instance, start negotiations with the essence of a matter and may later on come to talk about private things ("peach" model), while "diffusive" cultures are only prepared to deal with business matters after an interpersonal foundation has been built up ("coconut" model). "Diffusive" cultures do not separate the person from the matter and therefore, factual criticism cannot be separated from criticism concerning the person. Consequently, in Asia, criticism has to be brought up very discretely in order not to hurt anyone's pride or make loose anyone's face. "Specific" cultures concentrate on the negotiation matter while the person is not in the focus and personal relations may possibly develop rather after the business has come to a conclusion.

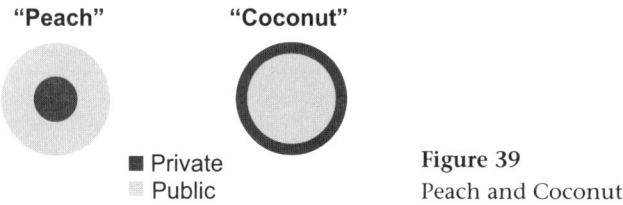

**"Peach"**  **"Coconut"**

■ Private
▦ Public

**Figure 39**
Peach and Coconut

*5) Achievement vs. Ascription*
The dimension polarity "achievement vs. ascription" describes the genesis of a person's status, if reached by individual performance or if reached by the existing background, i.e. if the person is member of a certain group, family, descent or if ethnic or religious factors play a role. While the American performance orientation is symbolized for instance by the legend of the dishwasher working his way up to becoming a millionaire, ascription-oriented cultures will pay a conspicuously great attention to (academic) titles, like for example in Austria or Russia.

[1]  After H. P. Rentzsch, 1999, 54, modified

*6) Way of Dealing with the Environment*
The way of dealing with the environment means for Trompenaars the degree of control that a person associates with nature – in the extreme, either subjection of nature or submitting to nature, i.e. fatalism (internal vs. external control). From this attitude will depend how much weight one would concede to either chance or luck in life, quite similar to the dimension pair "achievement vs. ascription". It is obvious that individualistically oriented cultures like the USA with their strong focus on the performance dimension will also, when dealing with nature, emphasize on the personal possibilities, while Asian cultures with their collectivistic orientation on background will also tend to a submission of the person under the environment.

*7) Way of Dealing with Time*
The way of dealing with time, Trompenaars' seventh dimension, refers – similar to Hall's concept – to the differences concerning living speed and rhythm or the claim for punctuality. Hall differentiates between a "sequential" and a "synchronous" orientation, this corresponding to Hall's pair of definitions of "monochronous" and "polychronous".

The selected above-mentioned contributions by Hofstede, Levine, Hall and Trompenaars today are fundamental for intercultural research, even if it remains open if the corresponding quoted dimensions are sufficient to describe the complexity of cultural diversity.

If we focus our attention now within intercultural management especially on the field of human resources management, the model of Evans, Lank and Farquhar demonstrates the culturally varying career paths that have led executives up to the top of an enterprise. The model distinguishes between Japanese, German, Romanic and English-Dutch career models in management.

## 6.4 Culture-specific Career Models

In the Japanese model, junior executives are being selected from the best of an age group. Within the Japanese long-term orientation, careers as well are planned on a long-term basis. During many years of trial and socialization phases, intensive trainings take place in short intervals. Regular and frequent evaluations are being made that correspond to the cultural attitude of uncertainty avoidance, and thereafter an intensive competition takes place which, after further years of qualifying proce-

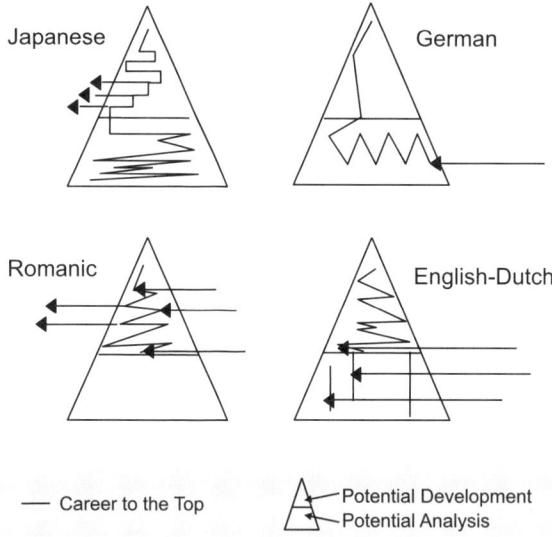

Figure 40 Culture-specific Career Models[1]

dures, will decide if a manager is msuccessful within a certain enterprise or if he should continue his career somewhere else ("up or out").[2]

In the Romanic model, executives are hired directly from the elite schools. In France, for instance, this is the usual way. In the phase of potential development, political circumstances and social networks as well as effective self-marketing are factors of success for the professional advancement. A clear system, like in the Japanese development model, however, is not apparent.

In the German model, during the identification phase, as a first step, through a horizontal job enrichment (model "trainee program"), a broad basis of specialist knowledge has to be acquired in several functions. This allows to determine the existing potential in each case, and the advancement during the phase of potential development then takes place out of this expert knowledge and the demonstrated efficiency.

---

[1]  After P. Evans, E. Lank, A. Farquhar, Managing Human Resources in the international Firms, London, Macmillan, 1989; Cp. C. Scholz, 2000, 537, modified

[2]  Cp. C. Scholz, 2000, 537

In the English-Dutch model, finally, the identification/analysis phase is generally oriented, without specially considering elites. Typical for the test phase are assessment centres or experience values resulting especially from the Anglo-Saxon empirical tradition.

## 6.5 The GLOBE Study

More recently, the "Globe Study of 62 Societies" (GLOBE being an acronym for "Global Leadership and Organizational Behavior Effectiveness" Research Program) is especially worthy of note. This is a research program originally designed by Robert House which, for 11 years (starting 1993) determined from 951 companies in 62 countries with the contribution of 170 researchers and 17.000 interviewees nine dimensions relating to organizational cultures and management styles.

### 6.5.1 Nine Cultural Dimensions

Under cultural dimensions are first of all stated two dimensions that we know already from Hofstede's and Trompenaars' studies, (1) uncertainty avoidance and (2) power distance. We therefore do not discuss these two dimensions here any more. The dimensions "individualism" and "collectivism" are divided by GLOBE further in (3) institutional collectivism and (4) in-group collectivism. Moreover, additional dimensions are introduced: (5) cross-cultural differences in gender egalitarianism, (6) assertiveness, (7) future orientation, (8) performance orientation, and (9) humane orientation. Amazingly enough, a dimension related to dealing with time is not mentioned.

*In-group Collectivism* describes the loyalty towards family and enterprise, while *Institutional Collectivism* refers to the degree of social participation or the distribution of resources for supporting and rewarding purposes.

> "In-Group Collectivism is the degree to which individuals express pride, loyalty, and cohesiveness in their organizations or families...Institutional Collectivism is the degree to which organizational and societal institutional practices encourage and reward collective distribution of resources and collective action."[1]

---

[1]  R. House, J. Mansour, Overview of Globe, in House, 2004, 12

On the basis of Geert Hofstede's dimension of masculinity, GLOBE develops the two dimensions *Gender Egalitarianism* and *Assertiveness*:

> "Gender Egalitarianism is the degree to which an organization or a society minimizes gender role differences while promoting gender equality. Assertiveness is the degree to which individuals in organizations or societies are assertive, confrontational, and aggressive in social relationships."[1]

With the extension by these two dimensions, the authors intended to avoid difficulties in interpretation that had occurred with Hofstede's studies related to masculinity. Although the research showed a significant correlation of Hofstede's masculinity score with GLOBE's assertiveness practices scale, it did not with the value scale. GLOBE also differentiates for instance between gender inequality and striving for success, a differentiation that is not mentioned in the masculinity score of Hofstede.[2]

*Future orientation*, finally, is a dimension that, according to the authors, corresponds only marginally to Hofstede's later used "long-term orientation" that was deduced originally from the "past, present and future orientation" by Kluckhohn and Strodtbeck[3], as a

> "...degree, to which individuals in organizations or societies engage in future-oriented behaviors such as planning, investing in the future, and delaying individual or collective gratification."

*Humane Orientation* also was deduced by the authors from Kluckhon's and Strodtbeck's dimension "human nature", as well as from the works of Putnam and McClelland, and it is to be understood as the degree "to which individuals in organizations or societies encourage and reward individuals for being fair, altruistic, friendly, generous, caring and kind to others."[4]

*Performance Orientation*, at last, is being defined as the degree up to which enterprises or society "encourage and reward group members for

---

[1]  Ibid.

[2]  Deanne N. Den Hartog, Assertiveness, in House, 2004, 431

[3]  F. R. Kluckhohn, F. L. Strodtbeck, Variations in value orientations, 1961

[4]  R. House, J. Mansour, Overview of Globe, in House, 2004, 13

performance improvement and excellence"[1], deduced by the authors from the working model "Need for Achievement" by McClelland.[2] Like in Hofstede's work, in the GLOBE project the values of the cultural dimensions were quantitatively visualized, additionally conglomerated in 10 societal clusters and a distinction was made between cultural "practices" (the way things are) and ideals of prevailing "values" (the way things should be)[3].

The GLOBE project's intention was to verify four hypotheses:

(1) "The societal system has a significant effect on organizational cultural practices."

(2) "The industrial sector has a significant main effect on organizational cultural practices."

(3) "There is a significant industry sector-by-societal system interaction effect on organizational cultural practices."

(4) "The industry sector-by-societal culture interaction effect on organizational culture practices will be a function of the isomorphic societal culture values."[4]

While the first hypothesis could be confirmed, saying that societal systems have the strongest effect on all nine cultural dimensions, for industry only a very weak influence could be proved and, therefore, hypothesis (2) could not be confirmed.[5] Interestingly enough, hypothesis (3) was partly confirmed as far as it related to 4 out of 9 dimensions, namely assertiveness, gender egalitarianism, power distance and uncertainty avoidance. The same happened to hypothesis (4), which was confirmed except as to power distance which did not prove to be significant. In total, however, it could be shown,

> "that societal system has the most significant and strongest effects on all organizational culture dimensions measured, whereas industry only weakly influences some of the measured aspects of organizational cultures across all societies."[6]

---

[1] Ibid.

[2] D.C. McClelland, The achieving society, Princeton, NJ, Van Nostrand, 1961

[3] M. Mansour, R. House, P.W. Dorfman, A nontechnical summary of GLOBE findings, in House, 2004, 29

[4] F.C. Brodbeck, P.H. Hanges, M.W. Dickson, V. Gupta, P.W. Dorfman, Societal Culture and Industrial Sector Influences on Organizational Culture, House, 2004, 658

[5] Ibid., 661

[6] F.C. Brodbeck, P.H. Hanges, M.W. Dickson, V. Gupta, P.W. Dorfman, Societal Culture and Industrial Sector Influences on Organizational Culture, House, 2004, 667

Hofstede's study already had made clear the strong cultural influence of the society on the organization, although he had been criticized because this study was limited exclusively to the IBM organizational culture. On the other hand, just this fact could also be seen as a confirmation of the primacy of the respective societal culture.

If we remember the statements concerning Robert House in Chapter 5, it is not amazing that House with the GLOBE study originally had in mind the generalizability of "charismatic leadership". House defines charismatic/value-based leadership as:

"visionary, inspirational, self-sacrificing, performance oriented"[1]

and he maintains it as the most desirable management style in most cultures. Among others, House here refers to the studies of B.M. Bass on transformational leadership[2] which comes very close to the concept of charismatic leadership. According to this, it has to be distinguished between executives

"that obtain followers by exchanging rewards...against performance with those followers that help reach their goals, and executives that, by a mutual compulsory association with their followers, succeed to shift motivation and morality reciprocally on to a higher level."[3]

The former type of leadership is called transactional, while the latter is referred to as transformational. House finds it interesting that in Bass' studies transformational leadership is understood as model of idealistic personnel management with an almost global cultural range:

"Although some fine tuning may be required, on all continents people's ideal leader is transformational, not transactional."[4]

---

[1]  H. Triandis, xix, in: House et. al., 2004

[2]  B.M. Bass, Does the transactional-transformational leadership paradigm transcend organizational and national boundaries?, 1997

[3]  J. Weibler, 2001, 333, own translation

[4]  In: P.W. Dorfman, R.J. House, Cultural Influences on Organizational Leadership, House 2004, 65

Three components of transformational leadership are seen as almost universal by Bass:

> "charisma, intellectual stimulation of followers, and individualized consideration toward followers."[1]

This strong focus on charisma in transformational leadership is exactly the reason why the charismatic leadership style is subject to criticism (i. e. inhibition of critical thinking and judging, missing development of own values, succession problems, etc.), as we have discussed already in the preceding chapter.[2]

In the GLOBE study, leadership is now defined as:

> "...the ability of an individual to influence, motivate, and enable others to contribute toward the effectiveness and success of the organizations of which they are members"[3]

although House knows very well that

> "there is no universal consensus on the definition of leadership."[4]

The implicit six dimensions of leadership examined in the GLOBE study are 1) "charismatic/value-based", 2) "team-oriented", 3) "participative", 4) "autonomous", 5) "humane " and 6) "self-protective" leadership:

## 6.5.2 Leadership Dimensions

*1) Charismatic/Value-based Leadership*
is the ability "to inspire, to motivate, and to expect high performance outcomes from others based on firmly held core values."

---

[1] Ibid.

[2] Cp. A. Brymann, Charisma and Leadership in Organizations, 1992, 174; J. Weibler, 2001, 336; C. Scholz, 2000, 957

[3] R. House, J. Mansour, Overview of Globe, in House, 2004, 15

[4] Ibid.

*2) Team-oriented Leadership*
"emphasizes effective team building and implementation of a common purpose or goal among team members."

*3) Participative Leadership*
"reflects the degree to which managers involve others in making and implementing decisions."

*4) Humane-oriented Leadership*
"reflects supportive and considerate leadership but also includes compassion and generosity."

*5) Autonomous Leadership*
"refers to independent and individualistic leadership attributes."

*6) Self-protective Leadership*
"focuses on ensuring the safety and security of the individual and group through status enhancement and face saving."[1]

GLOBE pursued, related to leadership, the examination of four theses:

"Hypothesis 1: Two leadership characteristics – Charismatic/ Value-based leader behavior and leader integrity – will be universally perceived as leading to effective leadership.

Hypothesis 2a: Leadership CLT [Culturally endorsed Leadership Theory] profiles, which are in essence profiles of prototypical leader behaviors and attributes, can be developed for each societal culture. These indicate which aspects of leadership are perceived to contribute to or impede outstanding leadership within that culture.

Hypothesis 2b: Societal CLT profiles can be aggregated into culture cluster CLT profiles indicating which aspects of leadership (found in Hypothesis 2a) are perceived to contribute to outstanding leadership for societal clusters.

Hypothesis 3: There will be positive relationships between CLT dimensions and societal culture dimensions that are conceptually similar or clearly related on theoretical grounds.

Hypothesis 4: There will be positive relationships between organizational culture dimensions and CLT leadership dimensions that are conceptually similar or related on theoretical grounds."[2]

---

[1]  All quotations from: R. House, J. Mansour, Overview of Globe, in House, 2004, 14

[2]  P. W. Dorfman, P. J. Hanges, F. C. Brodbeck, Leadership and Cultural Variation, The identification of culturally endorsed leadership profiles, House, 2004, 673ff.

The cultural factors of influence found out for instance for the leadership dimension "charismatic/value-based" are above all performance orientation, in-group collectivism and gender egalitarianism, each specified for "organizational level" (O) resp. "societal level" (S).[1]

The six dimensions of leadership are based on 112 sub-characteristics. 20 of these sub-characteristics are clearly classified as related to effectiveness, especially features like high performance orientation, trustworthiness, honesty, fairness, farsighted planning and acting, positive thinking, energy, ability to motivate, or team-oriented management style.[2]

These results support the hypothesis that there are universal characteristics of global leadership and they also emphasize the statement that such a global leadership is rather humane-oriented than business-oriented.[3] However, it has to be paid attention to the fact that these dimensions of leadership – like all dimensions ascertained on an intercultural basis – are relatively abstract and can therefore only be understood within the respective cultural context.[4]

Furthermore, the individual expectations on effective leadership and organization are primarily influenced by societal culture and only secondarily by the organizational culture, as can be seen from the GLOBE project.[5] Moreover, the fit between characteristics and behavior of an executive and the expectations on the employees' side on how they should be guided will influence leadership success significantly.[6] Concerning the question how far societal and organizational cultural practices and values do correspond to the expectations that successful executives are expected to meet, a considerable dispersion can be observed in the dimensions, and, when looking at authoritarian and autonomy-oriented management styles, even a very big intercultural dispersion becomes obvious, especially between Europe and Asia.

In total, the results of the GLOBE study do not encourage the attempt to pursue the model of an international "Global Manager" as described

---

[1] Ibid., 702
[2] F.C. Brodbeck, 2008, 2
[3] Ibid.
[4] F.C. Brodbeck, 2008
[5] F.C. Brodbeck, 2008
[6] R.G. Lord / K.J. Maher, 1991; Cp. F.C. Brodbeck, 2008

in the passage on organizational cultures in the present chapter, because the cultural heterogeneity is just too pronounced. F.C. Brodbeck is in favour of a model that would, according to practice, be oriented on the "Country Manager", preferably in combination with countries where cultures were not too heterogeneous.[1]

The GLOBE project is, since Hofstede's and Trompenaars' work, the most extensive study that is supported by a huge number of empirical data and that separately registers partial cultures, societal, organizational and branch cultures. Additionally, it even distinguishes between cultural practices and values. Hofstede did not do so, but had tried to derive values by questions on behaviour.[2]

While Hofstede's study – among other reasons – was also criticised because exclusively the IBM management had been interviewed, GLOBE covered more than 951 enterprises and three branches, namely finance, food and telecommunication.[3]

On the other hand, GLOBE only interviewed the middle management, thus facilitating comparability on the one hand, but impeding representativity on the other. The criticised equation between cultures and countries by Hofstede was countered by GLOBE through splitting countries and cultures. However, this approach could not be quite maintained throughout the study (for example separation Eastern and Western Germany, German and French speaking Switzerland, white and black population in Africa), and for huge areas like India, China and USA it is even completely missing.

House, originally, with his intention "to test the cross-cultural generalizability of charismatic leadership"[4] had pursued a rather culture-free approach which, however, could only partially be confirmed by the study. The core statements of the GLOBE results, finally, are the high influence of the societal culture on the organizational culture as well as the fact that leadership theory depends on the societal as well as the organizational culture.

Based on the GLOBE results, we may surely ask ourselves on our way to globalization how far this process will move further on and if at some

---

[1]  F.C. Brodbeck, 2008. Cp. M. Mansour, R. House, P.W. Dorfman, A nontechnical summary of GLOBE findings, in House, 2004, 52

[2]  Cp. Kutschker/Schmid, 2008, 730

[3]  R.J. House, M. Javidan, Overview of Globe, House 2004, 20

[4]  House, 2004, xxi

stage a global equalization of regional and cultural differences will have been reached. According to today's knowledge, a homogeneous global culture is not probable, although it can be assumed that during the years to come a further convergence will take place, especially to North American, Western European and Japanese cultures.[1]

Despite of the already existing results in the field of intercultural research, many questions still remain open. Apart from the heterogeneity of contents in the cultural dimensions postulated by different experts, criteria like, for instance, interaction and dominance still are not clear. When different cultures get in contact with each other, which one will become predominant? Are all dimensions to be considered as equal or are some of them more important than others? etc.[2]

With these remarks we will terminate our excursus into the international intercultural management. Even globalization will not be able to extinguish the roots of hundreds of years old national cultural archetypes and this, certainly, cannot be the objective of international management either. On the contrary, the cultural differences must be identified and taken advantage of. At least idealistically, the possibilities that open up by a strategy of internationalization on a mixed culture basis seem to be very tempting, even though putting it into practice can be expected to be complex and to require a long-term orientation.

The Italian astronomer Galileo Galilei (1564-1642) once put into perspective the geocentric world view of Ptolemy by supporting like Kepler the heliocentric standpoint of Copernicus and thus henceforth refusing earth the recognition as the centre of universe.

In a similar way, the cosmopolitan manager has to recognize the relativity of his own culture, and this perception can only take place – as Hegel's dialectics taught us – after a clear dividing line has been drawn to other cultures.

*"The end of all our exploring*
*Will be to arrive where we started.*
*And know the place for the first time."*

T. S. Eliot, Four Quartets

---

[1] Cp. P.W. Dorfman, R.J. House, Cultural Influences on Organizational Leadership, House 2004, 54

[2] Cp. M. Javidan/R. House/P. Dorfman/V. Gupta/P.J. Hanges/M. Sully de Luque, Conclusions and Future Directions, House, 2004, 723

# Disciplines of System Theory

The following deployment of systemic thinking out of interdisciplinary research hopes to prevent this theory from striving just for a utopistic humanistic ideal, with no basement in understanding human nature. We want to show interdisciplinary examples, which promote the aspect of self organization to use them later on for the transfer to human resources management.

## 7.1 System Theory as Interdisciplinary Approach

Before turning our thoughts to the question how Leadership can take advantage of system theory, we should start by defining what exactly "system" means within our context. Technical terms related to system theory are meanwhile used in many disciplines, and, very often, they are used quite ambiguously.

Maybe we should start with what the term should just not describe, namely system theory as an approach that in the sense of a nomenclature on sociology or environmental sciences just means the networking of groups, organizations, biological systems etc.

Our focus, on the contrary, will be to understand man as biological system with relatively closed operations (except for metabolic processes). These operations only formally are linked with the environment and the metabolic interactions. As regards their content, systems are determined in their objectives, reactions and interactions by their inherent order.

We will derive this more closely by following interdisciplinary aspects of system theory in order to show that our application of this idea to economic sciences is far from being arbitrary.

On the contrary, it seems obvious that if for instance biological and physical systems are to be understood in the systemic paradigm, corresponding conclusions also have to be drawn for Leadership. If we conceive man in the sense of the systemic approach, we have to adapt leadership and shape it differently to what was done up to now.

We may have to recognize that there are certain leadership styles that – even if variable, depending on the situation – offer only very limited possibilities for interaction face to face with extremely diversified individuals. We may have to refrain from understanding leadership as an informational instruction which, with the appropriate interaction, will reach the expected results concerning performance and motivation of employees.

Finally, we maintain that with system theory a complete "Copernican" turning point in leadership research is introduced that moves away from the focus on education, performance and behaviour of the executive, and turns towards the objectives, the needs and the motivation of the employees.

While the traditional leadership research has been considering the executive as pivot and consequently has been trying to improve his performance by management styles and techniques, system theory will make the system, i. e. the employee himself, the object of research.

The interdisciplinary statements relevant to the development of system theory show that it describes an understanding of biological systems taken up from life itself – and therefore from man himself – and that it certainly is not limited to only expressing a humanist ideal.

By promoting this understanding and making it productive as Systemic Leadership, we may expect to increase the performance and motivation of employees and thus the efficiency of enterprises. People who are offered the possibility to develop their talents and satisfy their needs will be more motivated and will achieve more, and their enterprise will take advantage of it.

Therefore, neither can it be question of maintaining an economically irrational ideal of man, nor should we remain captive of an economic compulsory rationality that does not sufficiently take into consideration the needs and motivations of man. Our objective should be, as Erich Fromm so perfectly put it, "to create a healthy economy for healthy people".[1] Systemic Leadership can make a contribution to reaching this objective.

In the following we would like to examine how system theory appears in different scientific disciplines and what paradigms become recognizable. For this purpose we will form different clusters which do not pursue the end in itself of originally presenting partial disciplines, but which orientate themselves by the central thread – as already mentioned, not by the historical central thread, but by the systemic one.

Accordingly, we will on the side of natural sciences, form subject clusters of the theory of evolution, biology, physics, cybernetics and chaos theory. On the side of humanities, we will form subject clusters of cognition science, philosophy, educational theory, therapy and sociology. Following this, we will examine closer some concepts in management theory that already now take into consideration systemic theorems.

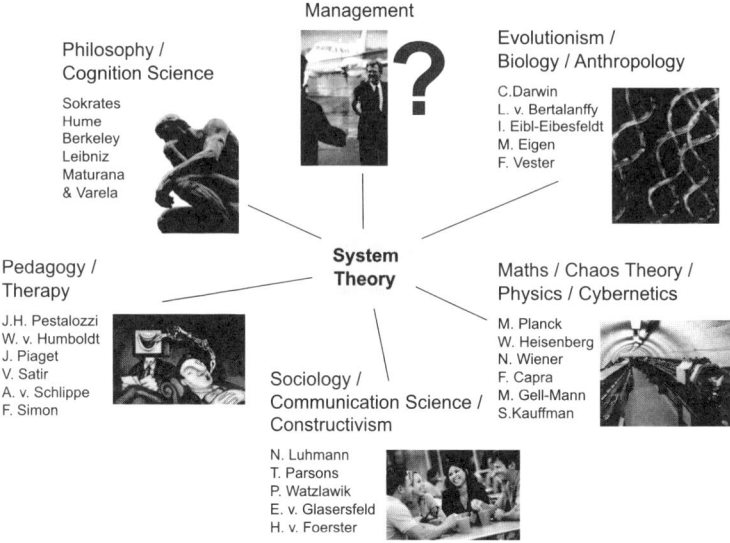

**Figure 41** Interdisciplinary System Theory

---

[1] E. Fromm, 1987, 169, own translation

## 7.1.1 System Theory and Biology

*Bertalanffy (1901-1972)*

The term "System Theory" appears for the first time in the works of the Austrian biologist Ludwig von Bertalanffy.

He called it "General System Theory" (GST) and dates its origin as follows:

> "I presented it [GST] first in 1937 in Charles Morris' philosophy seminar at the university of Chicago."[1]

Etymologically, the term goes back to the Greek Synistánai ("to put together"). The original idea is that systems cannot be understood purely scientific-analytically because the properties of its parts are not properties-in-themselves but can only be understood in the context of the greater whole.

This is also what we mean with the expression "The whole is more than just the sum of its parts", a thought that originally goes back to the Austrian psychologist Christian von Ehrenfels (1859-1932) and which became the key formula of systemic thinkers.

According to this, the essential characteristics of an organism or a living system are emergent qualities of the whole that cannot be found in any of its parts. As an example for this thought may serve bees and ants that cannot survive as individual beings, however, act when part of a certain quantity almost like the cells of a complex organism with a collective intelligence and adaptability, far superior to each single individual.[2] One can also express it like the biochemist Frederic Vester, – called the "father of networked thinking" -, who considers it a fact:

> "that complex systems on principle are something different from a pure coexistence of incoherent parts. Because each link of a system is in interaction with each other link. The system cannot be understood, let alone be shaped, without realizing this relationship ... dynamic systems, ...carry the program for their proper change within themselves. They are one whole of different units in interaction, an interactive system."[3]

---

[1] L. v. Bertalanffy, 1969, 90
[2] Cp. F. Capra, 1996, 34
[3] F. Vester, 2002, 15, own translation

Bertalanffy, however, with his understanding of a system, goes already far beyond the idea of system emergence when postulating not only the interdependence but also the inherent order of systems and thus predicts the new paradigm coming along with this and influencing our new understanding of man:

"Such a new image of man, replacing the robot concept by that of a system, emphasizing immanent activity instead of outerdirected reactivity, and recognizing the specificity of human culture compared to animal behaviour, should lead to a basic reevaluation of problems of education, training, psychotherapy, and human attitudes in general."[1]

At another place, Bertalanffy summarizes the difference between GST and the classic interpretation based on the attributes of objectives and purpose of an organism, thereby reminding of Aristotle's "Entelechy" (Greek Telos = goal and Echein = to have), according to which living beings always carry within them already the objective of their development:

"In human behavior goal seeking and purposiveness cannot be overlooked, even if we accept a strictly behavioristic standpoint. However, concepts like organization, directiveness, teleology, etc. just do not appear in the classic system of science."[2]

All forms of life, according to Bertalanffy, have to be understood as "open systems", thereby emphasizing their dependence on permanent energy flow and resources. He formed the term "flux balance", in order to express the coexistence of structure and change in all forms of life, an understanding where GST differed from the classical contemporary view of science.

"Conventional physics deals only with closed systems, i.e. systems which are considered to be isolated from their environment...Every living organism is essentially an open system. It maintains itself in a continuous inflow and outflow, a building up and breaking down of components...This is the very essence of

---

[1] L. v. Bertalanffy, 1969, 194
[2] L. v. Bertalanffy, 1969, 92

that fundamental phenomenon of life which is called metabolism..."[1]

Bertalanffy now adds to the criterion of metabolic openness of living systems, the attributes of activity according to the inherent organizational order of the nervous system. We should bear in mind that these thoughts were written down by him already in the 1960s, meaning that he was far ahead of his time and thus anticipated the actual scientific systemic thinking in its fundamentals:

> "We cannot say that...change comes from some outside agent, an input; the differentiation within a developing embryo and organism is due to its internal laws of organization...Even under constant external conditions and in the absence of external stimuli the organism is not a passive but a basically active system. This applies in particular to the function of the nervous system and to behaviour. It appears that internal activity rather than reaction to stimuli is fundamental. This can be shown with respect both to evolution in lower animals and to development, for example, in the first movements of embryos and fetuses."[2]

The concept of biological "drifting" is being anticipated by Bertalanffy, although at this point he still talks rather vaguely about adaptation by using remainders of image theory:

> "What is Truth is to be answered thus: Already the fact that animals and human beings are still in existence, proves that their forms of experience correspond, to some degree, with reality."[3]

> "It is not required that the categories of experience fully correspond in a certain way to reality whatever that means. It is not required that the categories of experience fully correspond to the real universe, and even less that they represent it completely. It suffices...that a rather small selection of stimuli is used as guiding signals...it is sufficient that a certain degree of isomorphism exists between the experienced world and the real world, so that the experience can guide the organism in such way as to preserve its existence."[4]

---

[1] Ibid., 39
[2] Ibid, 98f., 106
[3] Ibid., 241
[4] Ibid., 241

Chapter 7: Disciplines of System Theory

Bertalanffy did not yet clearly see that viability, i. e. the survivability, of an organism does not necessarily have to depend on the representation of the outer world – however small the degree may be – although the example he gives with the traffic light shows how far he has already moved away from a pure image theory – saying that an organism reflects within itself the structure of the environment – and how close he comes to the drift model.

> "The red sign is not identical with the various hazards it indicates oncoming cars, trains, crossing pedestrians, etc. It suffices, however, to indicate them, and thus red is isomorphic to stop, green isomorphic to go."[1]

The difference remains however that in Bertalanffy's example the organism recognizes symbols of the outer world and reacts accordingly (in this case the traffic light), while in the drift model even symbols as representatives of the outer world do not play any role. Because of its active self-organization the organism rather gets at some time to its limits which disturb the processes of the own structure, prevent them or even threaten its survival. According to this and to remain in the same example, a red traffic light could only be recognized after a collision with a car had taken place and future behaviour would connote the perception "red traffic light" and experienced threat. However, it would be possible that an organism survives although it interprets symbols completely wrong because the interpretation is subject to self-organization and not to a perception of symbols representing the outer world.

The terms which we use here, – "adaptation", "drifting", "viability", "open" and "closed" as well as "self-organization" – naturally raise many questions that will have to be clarified in the frame of the biological systemic discourse. For this, we would like to examine in a first step how evolution can be understood in a systemic sense.

The further the brain of a vertebrate is developed, the bigger are the areas in the cerebral cortex that cannot any more be assigned to clear functions like seeing or hearing. This enables vertebrates to react flexibly to evolutionary requirements. Different to insects or snails that rather respond to a stimulus by a fixed behaviour, the input in higher

---

[4] Ibid., 241

[1] Ibid., 241

animals is being worked on and modulated over many intermediate stages.

Accordingly, the respective reactions may vary greatly. While the original classical adaptation theory assumes that the reaction has been developing as an adaptation to environment and thus its success depends on how well the environment is being portrayed and recognized by the living being, biological system theory maintains that the success of the corresponding reaction is uncoupled from the adaptation to environment.

Thus, the decisive criterion would be if viability of the organism is given or not. The inherent laws of a living system are also to be seen dynamically and grow in the process of survival:

> "Even for the development of highly complex forms nature seems to lay down only few key data in the corresponding genetic material. It uses – after all, nothing else was to be expected – in a cybernetic way the knowledge of the associations and saves only few control instructions that determine the direction of the play. The final shape then emerges all by its own out of the connections of the system...Thus it is the laws inherent to the system that finally let every cell of our body know where it is situated and what task it has to take over."[1]

An organism is determined by its inherent laws and therefore it is to be understood as closed, while parallel at the same time – caused alone by the mere necessity of the metabolism – the formal opening to the environment is maintained. Living systems, therefore, are to be seen as closed and open at the same time. If they were purely closed, they would be in a homeostatic balance, which is not possible for a living system:

> "The equilibrium is a stable condition. There are no disturbances that could change fundamentally the distribution of probability in the system as long as the outside conditions remain constant. Therefore, information cannot develop in systems that are in thermodynamic balance."[2]

---

[1] F. Vester, 2002, 137, 142, own translation
[2] M. Eigen, 1987, 43, own translation

Chapter 7: Disciplines of System Theory

Not only openness and dynamic force have proved enhancing to evolution for living systems, but also the limitation of individual life cycles:

> "Growing old and dying has proved advantageous for the development of the species to such an extent that it became inevitable in the evolutionary process."[1]

Thus, as fundamental principles of selection and also of evolutionary progress, we may quote mutation, self-reproduction and the openness of living systems, as stated by the Nobel Prize Winner for Biochemistry, Manfred Eigen:

> "Mutations are the source of evolutionary progress. For this it is important that all mutants equally dispose of the ability of replication. Replication thus is an inherent autocatalytic characteristic of the whole class of molecules. For the dynamic behaviour, this means: growth and competition between all individuals capable of replication. The result of competition – no matter if the system as a whole grows or remains stationary – is selection. It takes care of an internal regulation of relative population figures – as regards quality like a chemical equilibrium, as regards quantity, however, different from it."[2]

## Eigen (*1927)

While, according to Darwin, organisms are developing by chance out of the molecular chaos by arbitrary mutations and natural selection, the probability that even simple cells could have emerged in this way within the period of time that is known to us as the existence of the world, is very small.

Manfred Eigen assumes a preparatory biological phase of evolution, during which selection processes appear on a molecular level as a special material quality inherent to chemical systems, i.e. the above mentioned "catalytic cycles". While for instance the microbiologist Louis Pasteur still postulated that life could only come from life – thereby not answering the question concerning the origin of life, but only postponing it – indications on connections and transitions between inorganic and organic processes appeared for instance 1828 in the works of the

---

[1]  M. Eigen, 1987, 113, own translation
[2]  M. Eigen, 1987, 255, own translation

chemist Friedrich Wöhler who succeeded to produce synthetically from the inorganic salt ammoniumcyanate the organic uric acid.

In the so-called neo-darwinism, the thought of gradual evolutionary change (Darwin) meets with the idea of a genetic stability (Mendel). Even if, according to Darwin (1809-1882), characteristics transmitted from parents to children get mixed and therefore become weaker, Gregor Mendel's theory explains that there positively are genes the transmission of which from generation to generation takes place without change in their identity.

This explains that random mutations remain in existence within a few generations and that they become either reinforced or wiped out by natural selection. According to this, any evolutionary deviation results from a random mutation, i.e. from genetic changes happened by chance which are then being followed by natural selection. If, for example, an animal requires a thick fur in order to survive in a cold climate, it will not react to this requirement by deliberately developing a thick fur. It will pass through all sorts of possible genetic changes and those animals where these changes lead by chance to a thick fur will survive and produce more offspring.[1]

The sexual reproduction process by which complete organisms keep being formed is not the only survival strategy of nature. The biologist Hans Driesch (1867-1941) found out that eggs of sea urchins regenerate whole organisms out of some of their parts. In his "Philosophie des Organischen" (1930), Driesch calls such systems harmonious equipotential and tries to prove that they cannot be explained mechanically. The power at the root of it was called by Driesch "vitalism", a purposefulness and inherent order of all appearances of life which Driesch saw in accordance with Aristotle's idea of entelechy.[2]

With the progressing cell specialization in more complex forms of life, the ability for self-repair and regeneration increasingly diminished. Flat worms, octopi, starfishes still today are able to regenerate almost their complete body from small fragments. Also, lizards, salamander, crabs, lobsters and many insects are able to have grow again lost organs or limbs. In higher animals, regeneration is limited to the renewal of tissue when healing injuries.

---

[1] Cp. F. Capra, 1996, 225
[2] Cp. S. Kauffman, 1999, 59

While Manfred Eigen derives selection from the existence of competition between individuals and thus makes competition in Darwinist tradition to the essential criterion for evolution, the Austrian systemic theorist and physicist Fritjof Capra, on the contrary, points out that cooperation is to be seen as much more important for viability than social darwinistic competition.

## Capra (*1939)

> "All larger organisms, including ourselves, are living testimonies to the fact that destructive practices do not work in the long run. In the end the aggressors always destroy themselves, making way for others who know how to cooperate and get along. Life is much less a competitive struggle for survival than a triumph of cooperation and creativity. Indeed, since the creation of the first nucleated cells, evolution has proceeded through ever more intricate arrangements of cooperation and coevolution."[1]

Or, as the biologist Lynn Margulis (*1938) put it:

> "Life did not take over the globe by combat, but by networking."[2]

According to Capra, the microbiological findings of Lynn Margulis as well as the works of the biophysicist James E. Lovelock (*1919) show that the narrow Darwinist idea of adaptation leads astray. In the whole living world, so he says, evolution does not let itself limit to the adaptation of organisms to their environment because the environment itself is shaped by living systems that, in their turn, again are able of adaptation and creativity.

> "So closely coupled is the evolution of living organisms with the evolution of their environment that together they constitute a single evolutionary process in which life has, quite literally, fashioned the environment to suit itself."[3]

---

[1] F. Capra, 1996, 243

[2] L. Margulis, D. Sagan, 1986, 29

[3] James E. Lovelock, 1991, 99, Cp. F. Capra, 1996, 227

From a biological standpoint, there are good reasons, when exploring life, not to rely on the anthropocentric point of view:

> "The speed with which drug resistance spreads among bacterial communities is dramatic proof that the efficiency of their communications network is vastly superior to that of adaptation through mutations. Bacteria are able to adapt to environmental changes in a few years, where larger organisms would need thousands of years of evolutionary adaptation. Thus microbiology teaches us the sobering lesson that technologies like genetic engineering and a global communications network, which we consider to be advanced achievements of our modern civilization, have been used by the planetary web of bacteria for billions of years to regulate life on Earth."[1]

## Dawkins (*1941)

The biologist Richard Dawkins (*1941) also draws our interest for understanding evolution away from man and towards the 'selfish' genes:

> "We are survival machines – robot vehicles, blindly programmed to preserve the selfish molecules known as genes...Without the gene's-eye view of life there is no particular reason why an organism should 'care' about its reproductive success and that of its relatives, rather than, for instance, its own longevity."[2]

While Capra does not see any reason for the existence of an evolutionary blueprint,

> "There is no evidence of any plan, goal, or purpose in the global evolutionary process and thus no evidence for progress."[3]

and Dawkins also does not share an anthropocentric understanding of evolution,

> "The idea that all evolution was aimed at producing Homo sapiens was certainly well rejected..."[4]

---

[1] F. Capra, 1996, 229
[2] R. Dawkins, 1989, xxi, 234
[3] F. Capra, 1996, 232
[4] R. Dawkins, 2005, 596

Dawkins still assumes a kind of development, even though not in the sense of an anthropocentric one:

> "Is there an evolution of evolvability?...I am suggesting a permanent and even progressive trend towards becoming better at evolving."[1]

Although Dawkins does not assume any development at the level of the organisms as Darwin once had done,

> "Recent forms are generally looked at as being, in some vague sense, higher than ancient and extinct forms; and they are in so far higher as the later and more improved forms have conquered the older and less improved organic beings in the struggle for life."[2]

but he does assume a development at the level of the macroevolution:

> "Evolution itself might be said to evolve. So far...progress has meant individual organisms becoming better over evolutionary time at doing what individuals do, which is survive and reproduce. But we can also countenance changes in the phenomenon of evolution itself. Might evolution itself become better at doing something – what evolution does – as history goes by? Is late evolution some kind of improvement on early evolution? Do creatures evolve to improve not just their capacity to survive and reproduce, but the lineage's capacity to evolve?"[3]

As criteria for an improved evolution capability Dawkins indicates survival and reproduction capabilities[4], and furthermore the segmentation, i.e. the modular, standardized construction methods of elements, for instance cells.[5]

This idea on Dawkin's part leaves many questions open. Competition in Darwin's sense is related to the corresponding environmental situa-

---

[1] R. Dawkins, 2005, 605,606
[2] C. Darwin, 2006 (1859), Recapitulation and Conclusion
[3] R. Dawkins, 2005, 605
[4] R. Dawkins, 2005, 606
[5] R. Dawkins, 2005, 609

tion in which some prevail over the others. To derive a general trend concerning successful modules for survivability would therefore make no sense because with changing times and environmental conditions also the criteria of selection can change. It would, as an example, also go against the statement of F. Vester, according to which it is not advantageous for evolution to firmly commit to key data in the genetic material (see above).

If Dawkins assumes whole module standards in the sense of a quicker and better capability to survive, the question may be asked if this thought is not contradictory to the paradigm of mutations being supposed to turn up disorderly and by chance. A selective mutability would limit the sense of mutation as to survivability.

Moreover, the question would arise if with this thought of Dawkins, the idea of teleology does not creep in, undercover so-to-speak, for is it not obvious that selective mutation inevitably means selection in a certain direction?

After having discussed some basic terms like mutation, selection or reproduction by presenting some examples, we should now like to go back to our considerations as to how the interaction of living systems with environment is to be understood.

As we have seen, in a closed system energy is to be understood as constant; in open systems, however, there is a permanent conversion of energy based on the ongoing metabolism. How can we imagine the ambiguity of the open condition (metabolism) and the closed condition (inherent order) of living systems?

Not all physical changes in an organism are to be seen as acts of perception, although even at the level of bacteria one can talk of a certain "perception":

> "Even bacteria perceive certain characteristics of their environment. They sense chemical differences in their surroundings and, accordingly, swim toward sugar and away from acid. They sense and avoid heat, move from light or toward it, and some bacteria can even detect magnetic fields."[1]

---

[1]  F. Capra, 1996, 268

Not all impulses coming from environment cause structural changes in organisms. It can be observed that they react only to a fraction of the stimuli to which they are subject and the effects do not necessarily show up immediately.

We see this for instance when, in a dream, we deal with perceptions occurred earlier in time or when our perceptive apparatus grasps more information than we are conscious of. Accordingly, in case of a memory loss, what seems to happen is that only the access to the engrams is barred although the perceptions have been saved.

However, what is essential for the thinking in systems is that when changes are caused, these are of a structural nature and not of an operational one. The operational inherent order of an autopoietic system ("Autopoiesis" from Greek Autos = self and Poiein = to make) is according to this not to be influenced causatively by environment:

"Since all components of an autopoietic network are produced by other components in the network, the entire system is organizationally closed, even though it is open with regard to the flow of energy and matter. This organizational closure implies that a living system is self-organizing in the sense that its order and behavior are not imposed by the environment but are established by the system itself. In other words, living systems are autonomous. This does not mean that they are isolated from their environment...Thus, a living system is both open and closed – it is structurally open, but organizationally closed...It does not react to environmental stimuli through a linear chain of cause and effect, but responds with structural changes in its nonlinear, organizationally closed, autopoietic network."[1]

Thus, an autopoietic system permanently undergoes structural changes while at the same time maintaining its own organizational structure. There is nothing new, however, in the thought of permanent metabolic processes taking place:

"Many of these cyclical changes occur much faster than one would imagine. For example, our pancreas replaces most of its cells every twenty-four hours, the cells of our stomach lining are reproduced every three days, our white blood cells are renewed

---

[1] F. Capra, 1996, 167, 168, 269

in ten days, and 98 percent of the protein in our brain is turned over in less than one month. Even more amazing, our skin replaces its cells at the rate of one hundred thousand cells per minute."[1]

What is new, though, resp. specific to system theory, is the thought that through the environmental effects only structural changes are being released without influencing in its content the operational changes of the organism:

> "These living systems are autonomous, however. The environment only triggers the structural changes; it does not specify or direct them...In spite of this ongoing change, the organism maintains its overall identity, or pattern of organization."[2]

This new understanding of life also revolutionized brain research in the 1970s. While up to that time the "computer model" in cognition science still was assumed, meaning that information processing were based on linear rules and would happen locally, it could then be shown that for instance after injury, the brain, in self-organizational manner, is able to delegate those functions that have broken down to different other parts.

The comprehension of systems following the pattern of self-organization not only gained acceptance in biology, but also in physics – if we only think of partial disciplines like cybernetics, thermodynamics, quantum physics or chaos theory.

## 7.1.2 System Theory and Physics

> *"Without Satan and God, the universe now appears*
> *the neutral home of matter,*
> *dark and light, and is utterly indifferent."*
>
> Stuart Kauffmann[3]

---

[1]  F. Capra, 1996, 218, 219
[2]  F. Capra, 1996, ibid.
[3]  S. Kauffman, 1995, 4

The cyberneticist Gregory Bateson (1904-1980) explained living systems as cybernetic control circuits and, at first view, we are reminded of the comments relating to biological homeostasis:

> "All biological and evolving systems (i.e. individual organisms, animal and human societies, ecosystems and the like) consist of complex cybernetic networks and all such systems share certain formal characteristics. Each system contains subsystems which are potentially regenerative, i.e. which would go into exponential runaway if uncorrected...The regenerative potentialities of such subsystems are typically kept in check by various sorts of governing loops, to achieve steady state...Such systems are homeostatic, i.e. the effects of small changes of input will be negated and the steady state maintained by reversible adjustment." [1]

Bateson was strongly influenced by the Austrian physicist Norbert Wiener who created a new partial discipline in physics, namely cybernetics.

> *"As a graduate student at MIT, I would occasionally*
> *find him asleep on the stairs, creating a real obstacle*
> *to traffic with his portly figure."*[2]

### Wiener (1894-1964)

> "We have decided to call the entire field of control and communication theory, whether in the machine or in the animal, by the name Cybernetics, which we form from the Greek κυβερνήτης or steersman." [3]

Here, the theories of cybernetics as well as of control circuits in general are still based on the classical perception of physics saying that order is linked to balance (for instance in crystals) and disorder is linked to imbalance (for instance turbulence). Thus, J.W. Forrester (*1918), founder of System Dynamics still understood the theory of control circuits not only as an adequate theory for the understanding of life, but also homeostasis as an ideal.

---

[1] G. Bateson, 1972, 447

[2] M. Gell-Mann on Norbert Wiener, 1994, 72

[3] N. Wiener, 1948, 11

The early idea of cybernetics as well as that of the early control circuits generally is characterized by the fact that these models of cybernetic control circuits did not yet contain the possibility of building new structures and behaviour patterns as self-organized processes and, therefore, processes like evolution, development or creativity could not be adequately explained:

> "In the new science of complexity, which takes its inspiration from the web of life, we learn that nonequilibrium is a source of order. The turbulent flows of water and air, while appearing chaotic, are really highly organized, exhibiting complex pattern of vortices dividing and subdividing again and again smaller and smaller scales."[1]

Still, the thought of an inherent order was already there, which Norbert Wiener had – as he said himself – taken from the theory of monads from the philosophy of Leibniz:

> "If I were to choose a patron saint for cybernetics out of the history of science, I should have to choose Leibniz...Though the monads reflect one another, the reflection does not consist in a transfer of the causal chain from one to another. They are actually as self-contained as, or rather more self-contained than, the passively dancing figures on top of a music box. They have no real influence on the outside world, nor are they effectively influenced by it. As he says, they have no windows. The apparent organization of the world we see is something between a figment and a miracle. The monad is a Newtonian solar system writ small."[2]

The so-called "monadology" in the theory of the German philosopher and probably last polymath G. W. Leibniz (1646-1716) was characterized by himself as follows:

> "One could call all simple substances or created monads as entelechies. Because they have within themselves a certain perfection... and autonomy...which makes them to sources of their inner activities and, in a way, to incorporeal machines."[3]

[1] F. Capra, 1996, 190
[2] N. Wiener, 1948, 12, 41
[3] G. W. Leibniz, Monadologie, 1998, 19 (18), own translation

Chapter 7: Disciplines of System Theory

If we now address the raised thought of open systems that are far from equilibrium, but at the same time show orderly structures, we have to talk about physics, and there about thermodynamics.

The Russian physicist and Nobel Prize Winner Ilya Prigogine (1917-2003) created in this context the term of 'dissipative structures' that, in a paradoxical way, seem to unite order and disorder.

In classical thermodynamics, dissipation (i.e. loss of energy during heat transfer, friction, etc.) used to be connected with waste. Prigogine's term of a dissipative structure, however, describes dissipation in open systems as a source of order:

> "According to Prigogine's theory, dissipative structures not only maintain themselves in a stable state far from equilibrium, but may even evolve. When the flow of energy and matter through them increases, they may go through new instabilities and transform themselves into new structures of increased complexity…The vast network of metabolic processes keeps the system in a state far from equilibrium and, through its inherent feedback loops, gives rise to bifurcations and thus to development and evolution."[1]

The maintenance of dissipative structures requires, as the name already suggests,

> "the permanent dissipation of energy, this being equivalent to the stationary production of entropy."[2]

Dissipative structures can be living as well as non-living systems. An example for a non-living system with dissipative structure would be a water swirl draining off in the bathtub. Although water is steadily flowing through the swirl, the form of the swirl remains stable.[3] Living systems, because of the metabolic processes, are also far from equilibrium and require

---

[1] F. Capra, 1996, 89, 172
[2] M. Eigen, 1996, 119, own translation
[3] Cp. F. Capra, 1996, 194

"a permanent influx of air, water and food from the environment by the system, in order to stay alive and to maintain their order."[1]

We may therefore say that dissipative structures are systems that are only able to maintain their identity by constantly staying open for the influences of their environment.[2] In Capra's view, the German physicist Hermann Haken reached with his statements on non-linear laser theory at the beginning of the 1960s quite similar results which describe laser light as self-organizing system far from equilibrium.

Haken's theory would show, so he says, that the laser has to be supplied with energy from outside so that it remains far from equilibrium, but that the coordination of the emission was being carried out by the laser light self-organizationally. In the sense of Prigogine, this is the description of a dissipative structure.[3]

Although Manfred Eigen treats as equivalent energy dissipation and emergence of entropy, this is no reason to see a contradiction between the statements of thermodynamics and evolutionary biology[4]:

"Sometimes people who for some dogmatic reason reject biological evolution try to argue that the emergence of more and more complex forms of life somehow violates the second law of thermodynamics. Of course it does not, any more than the emergence of more complex structures on a galactic scale...the second law of thermodynamics applies only to closed...systems. One crucial mistake made by those who claim a contradiction between that law and biological evolution lies in looking only at what happens to certain organisms and not taking into account the environment of those organisms. The most obvious way in which living systems fail to be closed arise from the need for sunlight as a direct or indirect source of energy."[5]

Accordingly, even cells can be understood as dissipative systems:

---

[1] F. Capra, 1996, 197
[2] Cp. Briggs/Peat, 1989, 139
[3] Cp. F. Capra, 1996, 109f.
[4] Cp. also Briggs/Peat, 1989, 139, or S. Kauffman, 1995, 21
[5] M. Gell-Mann, 1994, 372, 235,236

"Cells are not low energy structures. Cells hum along as complex chemical systems that persistently metabolize food molecules to maintain their internal structure and to reproduce. Hence cells are nonequilibrium dissipative structures."[1]

We may in fact assume that the evolutionary tendency consists in building more and more complex systems by self-organization, even in the macro area of galaxies, stars and planets[2] where because of the permanent physico-chemical change in the biosphere as well as because of the continuous development of the organisms, a real equilibrium will never be reached. On the contrary, there are orderly, dissipative nonequilibrium systems.[3] Here, especially the German physicist and Nobel Prize Winner Max Planck has shown that entropy is equivalent to the irreversibility of physical processes.

## Planck (1858-1947)

While the first law of thermodynamics states that energy can neither be produced nor destroyed and the second law says that an autonomous transfer of heat resp. energy is only possible from hot to cold bodies – never in the reverse order –, we have, besides energy, a further characteristic quantity which is entropy.

By using the term 'entropy', the second law of thermodynamics accordingly states that entropy may be produced, but never destroyed. Thus, entropy represents not only the status of the order of a system but also a measure for the irreversibility of a process.

Irreversible processes always come along with the production of entropy whereas in reversible processes entropy remains constant. In isolated systems, entropy can never decrease. The law of entropy increase does not limit itself to thermal processes alone but, on the contrary, according to Planck, covers all phenomena of physics and chemistry.[4] On further thought, the principle of entropy increase, on the one hand, predicts the heat death of the universe[5],

---

[1]  S. Kauffman, 1995, 21
[2]  Cp. M. Gell-Mann, 1994, 371
[3]  Cp. M. Gell-Mann, 1994, 372
[4]  Cp. D. Hoffmann, 2008, 27
[5]  Briggs/Peat, 2006, 200

*"Long after the sun will have shrunk to a white dwarf,*
*new stars will light up…after maybe 10 trillion years –*
*the universe will then be a thousand times its present age –*
*all stars will have ceased to exist."*

May/Moore/Lyntott [1]

on the other hand, from the irreversibility results a temporal one-way street, and in fact, only now time is actually introduced as determinant[2]:

"The second law [of thermodynamics]…introduced time and history into a universe which Newton and classical physicists had pictured as eternal. Because the equations of Newtonian mechanics are time reversible, physicists formed the conviction that at the basic level of matter there is no direction to time…Thermodynamically, things go in only one direction. Time is irreversible; it has an arrow."[3]

Further evidence for the self-organizational processes in nature can be seen in the micro world of quantum physics. Max Planck realized that the emission of electromagnetic radiation takes place gradationally in the form of energy packages (so-called "quanta").

The size of the realized quantum leaps between the stages is defined in accordance with "Planck's Constant", a physical constant established by Planck. Based on Planck's discoveries, quantum physics were founded, which then became an object of research by Albert Einstein, Max Born, Erwin Schrödinger and Werner Heisenberg and which revolutionized Newton's classical physics (with causality and determination) in three principles:

1) There is no continuity, natural processes accordingly do not take place continuously.

2) Natural processes, in the atomic world, are not predictable unambiguously. Contrary to for instance billiard where a certain stroke triggers off the ever same movement, an atom, constantly bombarded in the same way, will keep showing different reactions. Ob-

---

[1]  May/Moore/Lyntott, 2007, 146, own translation
[2]  Cp. M. Eigen, 1996, 177
[3]  Briggs/Peat, 1989, 135

viously, in microphysics, the same causes do not have the same effects, meaning that the principle of causality is suspended.

3) The elements of microphysics (atoms, electrons) do not have an unambiguous character, at times they are to be understood as wave and at times as particle. Therefore we cannot talk of an objective state of nature.

Especially this third principle has led the physicist, philosopher and Nobel Prize Winner Werner Heisenberg to the statement that with our physical experiments we, in fact, do not describe nature but only our understanding of nature, – in other words – ourselves.

## Heisenberg (1901-1976)

Observer and observed accordingly cannot be separated, and this statement releases science from its postulated objectivity in its classical understanding, thereby subjectifying it:

> "If from the atomic appearances we want to conclude on principles, it turns out that we cannot any more link together in principles objective processes in time and space, but – to use a more cautious expression – monitoring situations...In atomic physics we have learnt that the perceptions cannot any more be linked or put in order following the model of the thing-in-itself...In this way, as Bohr put it, the quantum theory reminds us that when searching for harmony in life, we should never forget that in the play of life we are at the same time spectator and player."[1]

By the "thing-in-itself", Heisenberg refers to the epistemology of Immanuel Kant where the "thing-in-itself" represents that part of reality that exists independently from the identifyer. With the thing-in-itself, therefore, also the objective reality is disappearing. This theorem, in philosophy, has already been formulated in the same way by George Berkeley (1685-1753) or David Hume (1711-1776).

By abandoning the classical position in physics, in quantum physics now the necessity arises to content oneself, instead of the determinist causality, with the possibility of calculating probabilities of occurrence.[2] Interestingly enough, this idea goes already back to the Greek

---

[1]  W. Heisenberg, 2006, 71, 68, 61, own translation

[2]  Cp. M. Gell-Mann, 1994, 6

philosopher Arkesilaos (315–241 BC) who in his general scepticism did not believe attainable anything more than probabilities. These, however, so he assures us, should be quite sufficient for our life.

While, in classical physics, it was possible to determine at the same time place and momentum of a certain particle, in quantum mechanics, as everybody knows, based on Heisenberg's uncertainty principle, this is not allowed. The more exact the place of a particle is defined, the less certain is its momentum. This situation describes a certain quantum state of one single particle – a state where the place is determined. In another quantum state, the momentum of the particle is exactly known, however the place cannot be determined.[1]

By the way, Heisenberg's uncertainty principle seems to contradict at first sight the more recent teleportation experiments of the experimental physicist Anton Zeilinger (*1945). Zeilinger has shown that two correlated quantum particles flying in opposite directions always remain correlated. This means that the impact on one particle also has consequences on the other particle even if both are far apart in space.[2]

If, however, as Heisenberg has shown, any measurement act already changes the condition of a particle, its state will never be ascertainable. Zeilinger points out that the uncertainty principle here shows two limitations that are not decisive for teleportation.

On the one hand, teleportation does not deal with the necessity to determine all information contained in the system by measuring it, on the other hand, in fact, an information does not have to be known in order to be able to transfer it. Accordingly, it would be best not to make any measurement at all while transmission is taking place:

> "...where actually do we want to get to with teleportation? We are, in fact, not up to determine the complete information contained in a system. We would be satisfied if teleportation just transmitted to the addressee the information characterizing a system. The crux is that we do not have to define this information. We do not even have to know it. It just has to be transmitted."[3]

---

[1] Cp. M. Gell-Mann, 1994, 139
[2] Cp. Briggs/Peat, 2006, 184
[3] A. Zeilinger, 2007, 90, own translation

Even if it is true that teleportation – at least because of the uncertainty principle – does not become theoretically impossible, unfortunately many reasons speak against the hope that "beaming" ever becomes practically relevant.[1]

It is interesting to note that the thought of quantum particles being linked, also contains an idea which is relevant for system theory as well as for chaos theory, namely the co-operation of all elements in a system resp. the coherence among all systems. In chaos theory, a "holistic" approach has become accepted which corresponds to the results in quantum physics:

> "It is common now to hear scientists talk of perspective reality instead of objective reality, of likely scenarios instead of deterministic outcomes, of useful models instead of permanent truths."[2]

The famous "butterfly example" in chaos theory, based on a thought by the meteorologist Edward Lorenz in the 1960s, not only expresses the coherence among all elements and systems but also the emergence of very complex structures from initially simple conditions at the start:

> "As the new aphorism goes, the effect of a butterfly flapping its wings in Hong Kong can create a rainstorm in New York. Suddenly...scientists became aware that in deterministic (causal) dynamical systems, the potential for generating chaos (unpredictability) crouches in every detail."[3]

> "The central idea is simple and is captured in the so-called butterfly effect: a legendary butterfly flapping its wings in Rio changes the weather in Chicago...this implies that the detailed initial condition – how fast, at what angle, and precisely how the starling flapped its wings – would have to be known to infinite precision to predict the result. But both practical and quantum considerations preclude such a possibility. Thus the familiar conclusion: for chaotic systems, we cannot predict long-term behavior."[4]

---

[1]  Cp. A. Zeilinger, 2007, 321f.
[2]  Briggs/Peat, 1989, 201
[3]  Briggs/Peat, 1989, 69
[4]  S. Kauffman, 1995, 17

The criterion of chaos, i. e. the unpredictability of events, resp. indescribability with determinants, yet, is not a criterion which would be based on the insufficient knowledge of the existing variables:

> "At first it may seem unfair, or at least an exaggeration, to call a weather system chaotic just because we can't predict it. If our ability to predict is faulty isn't that because we lack all the necessary detail or we don't have the right equation? The answer is no...because of the iterated nature of nonlinear equations (which represent the interconnected nature of dynamical systems), no amount of additional detail will help perfect the prediction."[1]

Chaos theory therefore has as a basic axiom the incalculability and unpredictability of effects, and this because of the incalculable quantity of variables.

> "[Henri] Poincaré discovered that with even the very smallest perturbation, some orbits behaved in an erratic, even chaotic way. His calculations showed that a minute gravitational pull from a third body might cause a planet to wobble and weave drunkenly in its orbit and even fly out of the solar system altogether."[2]

This is the reason why many chaos theorists refuse the assumption of determinist structures. Essentially, the refusal of determinism, however, is not a purely theoretical objection. Even in the classical Euclidean world, order and chaos go hand in hand. An example would be the number Pi for circle calculation which can never be determined exactly.[3]

In fact, it turns out that it is practically impossible to figure out the multitude of determinants in very complex systems, as can be shown for instance with iterative computer simulations:

> "Given the speed with which normal computers do iterations, predictability vanishes within a fraction of a second when highly nonlinear equations are concerned."[4]

---

[1] Briggs/Peat, 1989, 69
[2] Briggs/Peat, 1989, 28
[3] Cp. Briggs/Peat, 1989, 70
[4] Briggs/Peat, 1989, 73

In iterative (lat. iterare = repeat) computer simulations, the same operations are constantly repeated in a continuous feed back process. When the meteorologist Edward Lorenz simulated in his computer non-linear equations for the modelling of the earth's atmosphere, the iteration process belonging to the problem-solving method showed that even tiniest differences after arbitrarily high iteration processes led to huge differences and thereby to divergences that characterized weather systems of a completely different quality.[1]

While this aspect of chaos theory certainly lives up to the name "chaos" and seems to contradict the ideas of structure and determinism, at the same time, a second aspect – and paradoxical at that – can be observed in chaotic systems. Chaotic systems, when left to themselves, lead to the production of patterns and orders. This can also be calculated in computer simulations. Self-organizational systems that actively produce and maintain structures may also be simulated by recursive, iterative functions.

When calculating such functions, it becomes evident that some operations, after any number of iterations, show a trend to a certain, stable value. When continuing the operations, this value did not change any more, i.e. continued operations only produced redundant values in an iterative process:

"Formally expressed: The result of an arithmetic operation (Op) on a basic value ($X_0$) be $X_1$, thus $X_1 = Op(X_0)$. The same operation carried out on this first outcome results in $X_2$, formally: $X_2 = Op(X_1) = Op(Op(X_0))$ etc. until the self-referential function $X_\infty = Op(X_\infty)$ is reached."[2]

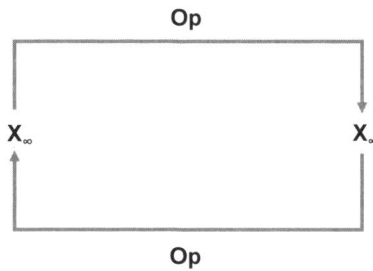

**Op**

$X_\infty$        $X_\infty$

**Op**

Figure 42
Iterative Process

---

[1] Cp. Briggs/Peat, 1989, 69

[2] F. Simon, 2007, 25, own translation

Independent from chaos research, mathematicians have also discovered the emergence and calculation of patterns in apparently disorderly structures, so-called "strange attractors". Attractors are values resp. conditions aimed at by a system. They are also known as "Mandelbrot set" and called after the French mathematician Bênoit Mandelbrot (*1924).

Mandelbrot invented, independent from chaos theory, in the 1960s a new geometry, the so-called "fractal geometry", for the description of chaotic attractors produced out of iterative methods. At first, he was not aware of the connection between fractal geometry and chaos theory.

An essential characteristic feature of aesthetic fractals is that their typical patterns repeat themselves in decreasing scales so that their parts have a form similar to the whole in any scale.

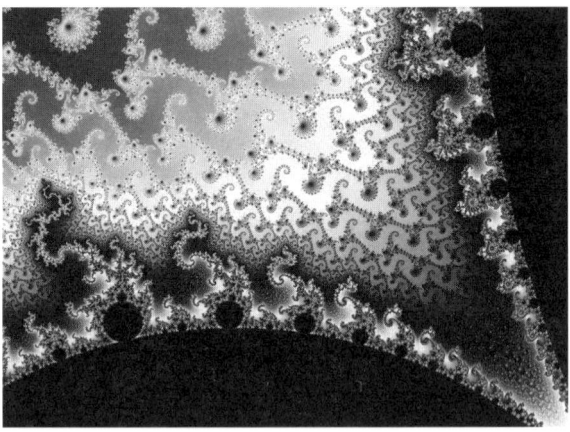

**Figure 43** Mandelbrot-Set

This self-similarity of the patterns that seems to repeat itself on every level of viewing may be described in its quality, however, fractals cannot be calculated as to their quantity, a characteristic which they have in common with the unpredictability of chaotic systems. The qualitative characteristics of the system behaviour, on the contrary, may very well be determined.

"Thus we see that chaotic behavior, in the new scientific sense of the term, is very different from random, erratic motion. With the help of strange attractors a distinction can be made between mere randomness, or noise, and chaos. Chaotic behavior is deterministic and patterned, and strange attractors allow us to transform the seemingly random data into distinct visible shapes."[1]

While we have seen in the statements relating to biological system theory that structural openness and operational closeness may very well go hand in hand, on the physical level the appearance of autonomous structures among chaos can be observed:

"Clearly a property of far-from-equilibrium chaos is that it contains the possibility of self-organization."[2]

It is interesting to see that these structures on the verge of chaos are definitely fragile on the one hand,

"The scientists of chaos have discovered that determinist systems which maintain themselves by oscillation, iteration, feedback, limit cycles (systems including most everything of interest to us) are vulnerable to chaos and face an indeterminate (unpredictable) fate if pushed beyound critical boundaries."[3]

but, on the other hand, just on the verge of chaos also show their highest performance as well as their ability to change:

"Complexity research suggests that self-organized, complex systems get their innovation ability, their creativity and their adaptability just from the fact that they operate on the verge of chaos...meaning that a system is in a critical condition so that the mentioned small changes may have a drastic impact."[4]

"It is almost spooky that such systems seem to coevolve to the regime at the edge of chaos. As if by an invisible hand, each adapting species acts according to its own selfish advantage, yet the entire system appears magically to evolve to a poised state where, on average, each does as best as can be expected."[5]

---

[1]  F. Capra, 1996, 133, 134
[2]  Briggs/Peat, 1989, 137, 138
[3]  Briggs/Peat, 1989, 76
[4]  F. Simon, 2007, 30, own translation
[5]  S. Kauffman, 1995 27

Complex, energetically open systems as well as dissipative structures accordingly emerge far from thermal equilibrium on the verge of chaos:

> "...the reason complex systems exist on, or in the ordered regime near the edge of chaos is because evolution takes them there...It is a lovely hypothesis, with considerable supporting data, that genomic systems lie in the ordered regime near the phase transition of chaos."[1]

Interdisciplinary chaos and complexity experts like the American biochemist Stuart Kauffman even place self-organization as evolutionary source at the same level as Darwinist selection.

*Kauffman (\*1939)*

> *"Here is no Panglossian world, or Hobbsian either.*
> *Perhaps here is the reality we have always suspected.*
> *Do your best; you will ultimately slip into history along*
> *with the trilobites and other proud personae in this*
> *unfolding pageant. If we must eventually fail, what*
> *an adventure to be players at all."*
>
> *Stuart Kauffman*[2]

> "...if the forms selection chooses...were generated by laws of complexity, then selection has always had a handmaiden. It is not, after all, the sole source of order, and organisms are not just tinkered-together contraptions, but expressions of deeper natural laws...I propose that much of the order in organisms may not be the result of selection at all, but of the spontaneous order of self-organized systems. Order, vast and generative, not fought for against the entropic tides but freely available, undergirds all subsequent biological evolution. The order of organisms is natural, not merely the unexpected triumph of natural selection."[3]

> "...If we, and past eons of scholars, have not begun to understand the power of self-organization as a source of order, neither did Darwin...Selection is not the sole source of order after all."[4]

---

[1]  S. Kauffman, 1995, 90, 26
[2]  S. Kauffman, 1995, 243
[3]  S. Kauffman, 1995, 8, 25
[4]  S. Kauffman, 1995, 92

Kauffmann points out that in biology it does not yet exist a theoretical framework relating to evolution that would be able to merge self-organization and selection.

Here, the question may arise if Kauffmann, at bottom, does not understand self-organization as criterion of mutation. The thought of structure existing even before any kind of selection has taken place also seems to resemble the thought of 'evolution of evolvability' by Dawkins who likewise considers possible the emergence of viability modules already before any selection has taken place.

Kauffman's self-organization, however, contrary to Dawkins, does not have any content and says for instance nothing about an improved evolution ability. Kauffman as well as Dawkins possibly have in mind an order that would already be inherent in mutation.

We have seen that Kauffmann as well as Dawkins both reject a teleological gradualism as Darwin still had seen it realized by selection. Both, however, only seem to schedule this process earlier, at the time of mutation, called in Dawkin's terms 'evolution of evolvability', and in Kauffmann's words 'self-organization'. Kauffman mentions two reasons that are against the assumption of Darwinist gradual selection:

> "The most important presupposition – and, indeed, one of the most important presuppositions of Darwin's entire thesis – is gradualism, the idea that mutations to the genome, or genotype, can cause minor variations in the organisms's properties – that is, in its phenotype...can all complex systems be improved and ultimately assembled by accumulating a succession of minor modifications?...Darwin's assumption...was almost certainly wrong. I does not appear to be the case that gradualism always holds. In some complex systems, any minor change causes catastrophic changes in the behavior of the system. In these cases...selection cannot assemble complex systems. Here is one fundamental limit to selection. There is a second fundamental limit as well. Even when gradualism does hold in the sense that minor mutations cause minor changes in phenotype, it still does not follow that selection can successfully accumulate the minor improvements. Instead, an 'error catastrophe' can occur. An adapting population then accumulates a succession of minor catastrophes rather than a succession of minor improvements. Even with selection shifting, the order of the organism melts silently away."[1]

---

[1]  S. Kauffman, 1995, 151, 152

While, according to this, Kauffmann's theory replaces the selective adaptation by autonomous structures already during mutation, we may ask ourselves how Dawkins can imagine the ability to evolve by evolution otherwise than as a feedback learning loop. If, however, learning does not take place on the level of selective adaptation, does it then not have to take place already during the mutation process? As Dawkin's thought of an improvement of the evolution of evolvability does contain a teleological direction, the question remains open, how this direction emerges, resp. what criteria contain the improvement. Kaufmann does not have this problem as he does not postulate a directional process, but only the existence of autonomy.

"Whence the order out of my window? Self-organization and selection, I think."[1]

This self-organization preceding any selection is called by Kauffmann 'order for free':

"If this argument is correct, metabolic networks need not to be built one component at a time; they can spring full-grown from a primordial soup. Order for free, I call it. If I am right, the motto of life is not We the improbable, but We the expected...most of the beautiful order seen in ontogeny is spontaneous, a natural expression of the stunning self-organization that abounds in very complex regulatory networks."[2]

Possibly, the radicality of Stuart Kaufmann's thoughts only becomes clear after one has realized that this means that any kind of adaptation to environmental circumstances is not decisive as selection criterion any more, but rather that systems, before any adaptation to environmental circumstances has taken place, develop their own inherent orders.

"Evolution may be impossible without the privilege of working with systems that already exhibit internal order, with fitness landscapes already naturally tuned so that natural selection can get a foothold and do its job. And here...may be an essential tie between self-organization and selection. Self-organization may be the precondition of evolvability itself. Only those systems that

[1] S. Kauffman, 1995, 185
[2] S. Kauffman, 1995, 45, 25

are able to organize themselves spontaneously may be able to evolve further. How far we have come from a simple picture of selection merely sifting for fitter variants. Evolution is far more subtle and wonderful."[1]

This thought really puts the self-organization of systems on the same level with the causal laws of nature. Evolution itself is thereby described as self-organizing. If we follow this idea further, remembering the thought of the philosopher J.G. Fichte (1762-1814) that man was nature looking at itself, the difference becomes relative between man and nature, system and adaptation to environment.

> "Nature within me becomes conscious of itself in the whole…In every individual, nature sees itself…This consciousness of all individuals combined accounts for the perfect consciousness of the universe of itself."[2]

If man and nature, because of their original own inherent order, do not differ from each other, the term 'adaptation' also looses its sense. Order thereby interacts with itself. By no means does interaction become redundant by that, as can be seen by the thought of the "Mem" of Dawkins, meaning a behavior that spreads out in a population.

> "Those categories are mutually defined in a complex reaffirming circle. How could it be otherwise? Having invented the categories, we carve the world into them and find ourselves categorized as well."[3]

According to Dawkins, the mems as the "new replicators of evolution" also range over the cultural achievements:

> "Cultural transmission is analogous to genetic transmission in that, although basically conservative, it can give rise to a form of evolution."[4]

---

[1] S. Kauffman, 1995, 185
[2] J.G. Fichte, 1962, 28, own translation
[3] S. Kauffman, 1995, 300. Cp. also R. Dawkins, 1987
[4] R. Dawkins, 1989, 189

By now at the latest, when referring to the cultural evolution, we have reached the fields of philosophy and cognitive sciences where we now want to see how the scientific expositions for the understanding of biological and physical systems may be applied to our human self-conception. It is obvious that, as a first step, we should consult cognitive sciences, the task of which it is to examine the methods of operation of the human brain.

### 7.1.3 System Theory and Cognitive Science

As early as in the 1950s scientists started to construct machine models of binary networks. They observed that in most of the networks, after a short time of arbitrariness some regular patterns appeared. This spontaneous appearance of order was called self-organization.[1]

While cognitive sciences were making an effort to understand and describe human intelligence, it became quickly clear that human intelligence is completely different from the artificial intelligence of machines. The human nervous system, in fact, does not process information but is engaged in a dialogue with its environment, thus continuously modulating its own structure.[2]

It would therefore be inadequate to consider the brain as a data-processing computer in the sense of a trivial machine.[3] While trivial systems are analytically definable, determined and therefore predictable, non-trivial systems work analytically indeterminable and unpredictable.

**Figure 44** Trivial System

In a trivial system, an information (I) leads to an operation (O) of the system, thus finally bringing about a result (E of I) dependent on the original information.

---

1 Cp. F. Capra, 1996, 83
2 Cp. F. Capra, 1996, 68
3 Cp. F. Capra, 1996, 204

The machine as well as the computer system are useful for us in so far as the results of the operations are predictable and not arbitrary.

Man, as well as for instance the environment, however, as living systems, are to be understood as non-trivial, i.e. – if we want to quote the extremely uncharming example from Gregory Bateson – there is a big difference if we kick off a billiard ball or if we kick a dog, because in the latter case the reaction of the living system is not predictable.[1] From the original information that has been fed into the living system, the result, i.e. the reaction, cannot be predicted.

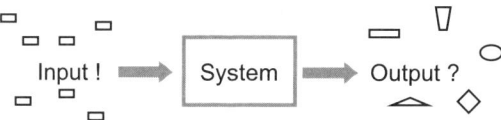

**Figure 45** Non-trivial System

As already mentioned, from brain research we know in the meantime that our brain works as network and that individual functions are not necessarily locally limited. After accidents, it could be shown that tasks can also be taken over by other brain areas, this finding being in favour of the cognitive self-organization.[2]

In this context, much speculation has been going on concerning the fundamental difference between artificial and human intelligence, especially on the question if it will ever be possible to shape artificial intelligence after the human one, as expressed in the idea of the "replicants" in the science fiction movie "Blade Runner".

The frequently stated difference between man and machine whereby man would give himself his own purpose and meaning in life while machines would only be programmed, cannot be maintained with the thought of an supposed determinism.

After all, we might understand determinism as a kind of programming. In the same way the reasoning that man felt free and not at all deter-

---

[1] G. Bateson, 1972, 409
[2] Cp. F. Capra, 1996, 71

mined[1], cannot be classified as difference because this also might have been programmed.

There is, however, one difference between man and machine that cannot be removed. Independent of the question if technical-practically it will ever be possible to construct machines similar to man, such "replicants" will always be different from man by the quality that replicants do know their creator resp. their programmer.

Is self-organization therefore principally programmable? Principally yes, in the same way as the random generator of a chess computer may be programmed. Consequently, theoretically, with sufficient knowledge of the operating variables, a deterministic system is unfailingly to be assumed when dealing with living or non-living systems.

The machine follows its artificial program, man follows his natural program. The range of possible behaviour of both is theoretically at any time predictable and already determined before any realization has taken place, even if, in practice, as we have seen with the help of quantum physics and chaos theory, the possibilities may today not be describable, resp. we are only able to indicate probabilities of occurrence.

For the Chilean cognition scientist Francisco Varela, the re-orientation of cognition sciences away from the input system of trivial machines toward a self-organized system is equivalent to the renunciation of theories that take as a basis an epistemological image theory of the environment (representation) in living systems:

> "These concepts imply three ontologically as well as epistemologically consequential assumptions: 1. The world is preset. 2. Our cognition refers to this world – even though often only to a part of it. 3. We perceive this preset world in such a way that we reflect its features and then act on the basis of these reflections."[2]

Varela rather sets as quintessence of his conception of the brain the spontaneous activity in contrast to the representation of the outer environment as basic pattern of living systems:

---

[1]  Cp. for instance "Genesis und Geltung" by R. Spaemann, 1984, 73

[2]  S.J. Schmidt, in F.J. Varela, 1990, 11, own translation

"The brain constantly brings forth worlds in the process of viable stories of creatures: it determines worlds instead of reflecting them. According to this opinion, viability replaces in the epistemological discourse ideas of adequacy."[1]

"The actual challenge…in this new orientation lies in the fact that it questions the most deep-rooted basic assumption indeed of our scientific tradition: that the world as we experience it is independent from the experiencing subject."[2]

## Varela (1946-2001) and Maturana (*1928)

Francisco Varela and Humberto Maturana, the latter also Chilean neurobiologist and philosopher, have developed together, based on their research of the functional principles of the brain, a model of operational closed systems which they then transferred to biological systems in general. They called this self-organization "autopoiesis".[3]

A quickly plausible example for the fact that with our perception we do not take in the reality around us as it is independent from us, but in accordance with our recognizing apparatus, has been shown by Varela referring to colours:

"An…example is the world of colours as we see them every day. Colours and their effects are so present everywhere in our life that we are tempted to assume that the colours that we see are like the world is. Normally, we believe that colour is part of the wavelength of the light reflected from objects, which we take up and handle as important information. However, often enough it has been explained in detail that the colour perceived of an object is to a great extent independent of the wavelength that strikes the eye. Instead, a complex process (that is only partially understood) takes place, in the course of which manifold neuron groups of the brain cooperate and in which their activities are set off against each other…All we can say is that our world of colours is viable: it is effective because in the biological sense we have survived."[4]

---

[1] Ibid.
[2] F.J. Varela, 1990, 97, own translation
[3] See above, Chapter 7.1.1
[4] F.J. Varela, 1990, 106, own translation

Varela here points out that for the survivability not necessarily a correct image (representation) of our environment is required. According to him, what is essentially decisive for living systems is if with their corresponding perception they are able to survive.

"The basic point therefore is that cognitive capabilities are interlaced with a life history, like a path that does not exist as such but only emerges in the process of walking. Therefore, my view of cognition is not that it solves problems with the help of representations, but that it creatively makes emerge a world whose only required precondition is that it allows successful actions: it ensures the continuation of the existence of the concerned system with its specific identity."[1]

If the criterion for the ability to evolve of living systems is indeed viability and not adaptability, then we cannot talk about a linear, optimal adaptability scale:

"There is no survival of the better adapted, there is only a survival of the adapted. Adaptation is a question of necessary preconditions that can be complied with in many different ways, whereas there is no one best way to meet a criterion that would have to be looked for beyond survival. The differences between the organisms reveal that there are numerous structural ways in which living organisms come into being, and not the optimization of a relation or a value."[2]

Varela and Maturana also turn their back on the Darwinist concept of a gradual adaptation:

"What we propose here is that evolution occurs as a phenomenon of structural drift under ongoing phylogenic selection. In that phenomenon there is no progress or optimization of the use of the environment, but only conservation of adaptation and autopoiesis. It is a process in which organism and environment remain in a continuous structural coupling...Nor is that guiding force needed to explain the directionality of the variations in a lineage, nor is it the case that some specific quality of living beings is being optimized."[3]

---

[1]  F.J. Varela, 1990, 110, own translation
[2]  Maturana/Varela, 1984, 125, own translation
[3]  Maturana/Varela, 1987, 115, 117

In fact, every kind of survivability is to be considered as equal:

> "Note...that there are many structural variations capable of producing individuals that can survive in a given environment. All these variations, as we saw before, are equally adapted. They are capable of continuing the lineage to which they belong in their particular environment, whether it is changing or not, at least for some thousands of years."[1]

From a phylogenetic point of view, the criterion for survivability is replicability:

> "...there are lineages that disappear, revealing that the structural configurations that characterized them did not enable them to conserve the organization and adaptation needed for their continuity. In the process of organic evolution, once the essential ontogenetic requisite of reproduction is fulfilled, everything is made possible."[2]

In the sense of a structural drifting, i.e. in the sense of co-evolution, living system and environment move side by side, and to get the idea across, Maturana and Varela introduce an analogy with the drive of a submarine boat:

> "Imagine a person who has always lived in a submarine. He has never left it and has been trained how to handle it. Now, we are standing on the shore and see the submarine gracefully surfacing. We then get on the radio and tell the navigator inside: 'Congratulations! You avoided the reefs and surfaced beautifully. You really know how to handle a submarine.' The navigator in the submarine, however, is perplexed: 'What's this about reefs and surfacing? All I did was push some levers and turn knobs and make certain relationships between indicators as I operated the levers and knobs. It was all done in a prescribed sequence which I'm used to. I didn't do any special manoeuvre, and on top of that, you talk to me about a submarine. You must be kidding!'"[3]

---

[1] Maturana/Varela, 1987, 107
[2] Maturana/Varela, 1987, 107
[3] Maturana/Varela, 1987, 136, 137

We have to see living systems as operationally closed because of their autonomy, but structurally open because of their metabolic dependence on the environment. In the sense of a non-trivial machine, one therefore cannot talk of a linear information reception of environmental influences by the system. Maturana and Varela, accordingly, prefer not to talk of information but of perturbation, since the living system is perturbed by the environment in the execution of its autonomous operations (operationally closed):

> "...the nervous system's organization is a network of active components in which every change of relations of activity leads to further changes of relations of activity. Some of these relationships remain invariant through continuous perturbation both due to the nervous system's own dynamics and due to the interactions of the organism it integrates."[1]

Because of the perturbation, therefore, the result, the reaction of the living system is not predictable and living systems are being influenced perturbatively by their environment as well as vice versa, this being called by the authors "structural coupling",

> "...it is the structure of the living being that determines what change occurs in it. This interaction is not instructive, for it does not determine what its effects are going to be. Therefore, we have used the expression 'to trigger' an effect. In this way we refer to the fact that the changes that result from the interaction between the living being and its environment are brought about by the disturbing agent but determined by the structure of the disturbed system. The same holds true for the environment: the living being is a source of perturbations and not of instructions...we...see between the structure of the environment and that of the unity a compatibility or congruence. As long as this compatibility exists, environment and unity act as mutual sources of perturbation, triggering changes of state. We have called this ongoing process 'structural coupling'."[2]

while, at the same time, organism and environment remain operationally closed, i. e. independent from each other:

---

[1] Maturana/Varela, 1987, 164
[2] Maturana/Varela, 1987, 95, 99

"Structural coupling is always mutual; both organism and environment undergo transformations."[1]

With regards to philosophy, Maturana and Varela postulate a concept that neither follows an epistemological solipsism (lat: solus = alone, ipse = self) nor does it follow representationism (realism):

"...the operational closure of the nervous system tells us that it does not operate according to either of the two extremes: it is neither representational nor solipsistic. It is not solipsistic, because as part of the nervous system's organism, it participates in the interactions of the nervous system in its environment. These interactions continuously trigger in it the structural changes that modulate its dynamics of states. In fact, this is the basis of why, as observers, we see animal behavior in general as being in line with its circumstances and why animals do not behave as though they were following their own leader independently of the environment. This is so despite the fact that, for the operation of the nervous system, there is no inside or outside, but only maintenance of correlations that continuously change...Nor is it representational, for in each interaction it is the nervous system's structural state that specifies what perturbations are possible and what changes trigger them. It would therefore be a mistake to define the nervous system as having inputs or outputs in the traditional sense. This would mean that such inputs or outputs are part of the definition of the system, as in the case of a computer or other machines that have been engineered. To do this is entirely reasonable when one has designed a machine whose central feature is the manner in which we interact with. The nervous system (or the organism), however, has not been designed by anyone; it is the result of a phylogenic drift of unities centered on their own dynamics of states. What is necessary, therefore, is to recognize the nervous system as a unity defined by its internal relations in which interactions come into play only by modulating its structural dynamics, i.e., as a unity with operational closure. In other words, the nervous system does not pick up information from the environment, as we often hear. On the contrary, it brings forth a world by specifying what patterns of the environment are perturbations and what changes trigger them in the organism. The popular metaphor of calling the brain an information-processing device is not only ambiguous but patently wrong."[2]

---

[1]  Maturana/Varela, 1987, 102

[2]  Maturana/Varela, 1987, 169

The reference to the philosophical solipsism makes us arrive at the principal question of how system theory should be imagined epistemologically. And with this, we have definitely arrived at philosophy.

## 7.1.4 System Theory and Philosophy

> *"Nasreddin was sitting by the river side when*
> *someone called from the other side of the river:*
> *"How can I get here to the other side?"*
> *Nasreddin replied: "But you are on the other side!"*

*Nasreddin*[1]

While Fritjof Capra denotes the so-called Santiago theory of Maturana and Varela as first scientific system that overcomes the Cartesian separation[2], we can also appreciate the philosophical initiation of these thoughts by George Berkeley or David Hume. Apart from the scientific genesis, they even go further with regards to the ontogenetic validity for the living system by already anticipating the process-orientation as well as the entelechy of the individual.

The idea of cognition being dependent on the recognizing subject can already be found in the well-known Homo-Mensura principle of the sophist Protagoras (480-410 BC) – a philosopher preceding Socrates – saying that man is the measure of all things. Universally valid truth, according to Protagoras, does not exist and his relativism is also illustrated by his statement that the same not even can be true for the same person at different times, because at different times a person will every time be another one.[3]

Protagoras here already expresses the process-related comprehension of a continuously changing existence that cannot be brought together with a stable concept of our identity.

---

[1] In: G. Frank (Ed.), "Der Schelm vom Bosporus. Anekdoten um Nasreddin Hodscha". Edition Orient, 1994, own translation

[2] Capra here refers to the dualistic separation of the spiritual (res cogitans) and the substantial world (res extensa) as outlined by the French philosopher René Descartes (1592-1650), a philosophical view of the world that essentially influenced our entire contemporary (especially scientific) thinking. Cp. Descartes, Meditationes de prima philosophia, 1641

[3] Cp. H. J. Störig, 1981, 152; K. Vorländer, 1990, Vol. 1, 152

A systematic demonstration of the 'second Copernican turn', moving man again into the centre, can be found in the cognition theory of the Scottish philosopher David Hume. What makes his philosophy so very charming is that initially and in best Anglo-Saxon empiricist tradition, he has not at all in mind to found a subjectivism. Rather, Anglo-Saxon tradition in reality aims at granting priority to sensual experiences.

While subjectivism (idealism) in philosophy always has been assuming the primacy of consciousness, considering everything else, environment, reality and fellow men in the extreme of solipsism (lat: solus = alone, ipse = self) as creation of consciousness, objectivism (realism) claims an outside world independently existing from and recognizable by the subject.

As far as empiricism bases its cognition on the sensual experience of reality, it is initially realistic and objective. However, in the course of further reflection one has to realize that, when logically thinking through this idea, an inversion to subjectivity and finally also a dissolution of the subject becomes apparent, just in the sense that Protagoras insinuates it, i. e. as a flowing process of being.

The subjectivist return of the world into spirit in the sense of the already mentioned second Copernican turn, by the way, is in fact neither a return nor an occidental ethno-centred philosophy. In Buddhism already, up to the mysticism of old Egypt, man has been considered as microcosm of the macrocosm:

> *"These realms are not come from somewhere outside [thyself].*
> *They come from within…They issue from within there,*
> *and shine upon thee. The deities, too, are not come from*
> *somewhere else: they exist from eternity within the faculties of*
> *thine own intellect. Know them to be of that nature."*
>
> The Tibetan Book of the Dead[1]

Also, in Buddhism for instance, no epistemic realism can be found, rather things as well as man are not more than "Maya" (world of appearance) and Buddhism also does not assume a constant subject. Subject is seen as a non-real illusion.[2]

---

[1] (Comp. and ed. by Evans-Wentz), 1960, 121
[2] Cp. F. Capra, 1996, 333f.

If we go back to the occidental tradition and the further development of the Homo-Mensura Principle by Protagoras we can observe in the 13th and 14th centuries of the middle age the preparations for empiricism by the so-called "dispute over universals" and the concept of the nominalism. The point was if our general terms (universals) like "house", "tree" or "man" have an equivalent in reality, or if, strictly speaking, we are dealing with names only (lat. "nomen", therefore called "nominalism").

If we realize that with one and the same general term we describe many different things with different features, it becomes clear that the general term "house" for instance is not sufficient to describe a particular real house, but that it is just a kind of generic term for all houses. We therefore have to add many more attributes in order to be able to describe concrete individual things in differentiation from others.

With this, nominalism already renounces the outer world and turns to the subject, postulating that our general terms do not portray reality but are just to be understood as the building of categories of a subject.

David Hume adopts this nominalism. Different from idealistic philosophies which understand the world a priori as emanation of the subject, like represented for instance by Fichte, Leibniz or Schopenhauer, empiricist philosophy is very interesting because the turn into the subject is effected so-to-speak unavoidably. It occurs because of the stringency of the thoughts and pursues, in its original effort to found cognition onto the sensual outer everyday perception, just exactly a sober, scientific, realistic approach. On the other hand, we have chosen David Hume's epistemology because, among the empiricist concepts, it is at the same time the logically most stringent one as well as the most radical one. Let us accompany this mental adventure for a short while.

## Hume (1711-1776)

Hume, at the beginning, asks himself how our thinking comes into being. On the one hand he discovers impressions, on the other hand, ideas. The impressions are divided by him into sensory perceptions (sensations) and self-perception (reflections).

The same had been done before by John Locke (1632-1704), also a representative of empiricism. Ideas differ from impressions insofar as the former have a higher degree of liveliness. This does not mean anything else but that reality and dream cannot be distinguished by their intensity and that, qualitatively, they are equal. Hume therefore calls the ideas faint images of the sensory perceptions.[1]

For Hume as well as for the whole empiricist tradition it is important that the sensory perceptions always precede our ideas, it can never be vice versa. This axiom again was already set up by John Locke. Accordingly, nothing can be in our thoughts that does not come from our senses ("Nihil est in intellectu quod non prius fuerit in sensu").[2]

This thought has far-reaching consequences because what it means is that we are not able to think anything that is not based on sensory perceptions. And what if we thought for instance of Pegasus, the winged horse? Hume would say that all we do here was to combine two single sensory perceptions, that of a horse and that of wings, and put them together.

The same happens if we think of cold fire or of 'nothing' or infinity. Thus, 'nothing' cannot be really thought of, instead, we then think for instance of a white space, etc. and if we try to think of infinity, all we can do is to string together again and again finite sensory sections.

After Hume has proven that all our thinking is based on our sensory perception, he passes on to the question where our sensations themselves come from. While philosophical traditions like idealism, subjectivism or solipsism assume that the environment around the subject is being created by the subject, that it depends on the subject or even, like in solipsism, only exists in the subject, empiricism has once more to be distinguished from all this because the objects of the environment, the so-called material substances, are here dissolved as well.

The idea that, based on our sensory perception, we actually never perceive substances, material things and the same, was already conceived by the Irish Bishop George Berkeley (1685-1753) when he pointed out that haptics and optics in our perception do not correlate:

> "But if we take a close and accurate view of things, it must be acknowledged that we never see and feel one and the same object. That which is seen is one thing, and that which is felt is another. If the visible figure and extension be not the same with

---

[1]  D. Hume, A Treatise of Human Nature, 1978, 1

[2]  This thought was satirized by the idealist Leibniz who added: "Nisi intellectus ipse" (except intellect itself).

the tangible figure and extension, we are not to infer that one and the same thing has diverse extensions. The true consequence is that the objects of sight and touch are two distinct things."[1]

With persons born blind who later recovered their eyesight, so he states, one could observe that the earlier acquired tactile impressions are not being linked with the newly acquired visual impressions, because they are not acquired in a temporal coincidence.[2]

Even if we rely solely on one sensory channel, we should better not trust these sensory experiences, as can be demonstrated by false perceptions of the tactile kind (a very cold hand realizes lukewarm already as hot) or of the visual kind (for instance our purely visual impression on the size of distant objects). The Lebanese poet Khalil Gibran (1883-1931) once expressed this idea beautifully:

### The Eye

*Said the Eye one day, "I see beyond these valleys a mountain*
*veiled with blue mist. Is it not beautiful?"*
*The Ear listened, and after listening intently awhile, said,*
*"But where is any mountain? I do not hear it."*
*Then the Hand spoke and said, "I am trying in vain to feel it*
*or touch it, and I can find no mountain."*
*And the Nose said, "There is no mountain, I cannot smell it."*
*Then the Eye turned the other way, and they all began to talk*
*together about the Eye's strange delusion. And they said,*
*"Something must be the matter with the Eye."*

K. Gibran, The Madman[3]

This leads Berkeley to affirm that an outer world independent from our perception and our thinking did not exist. The being of things only consisted in their being perceived (esse est percipi, lat. = being is being perceived).

This leads to some conclusions that are contradictory to our common sense. If the existence of reality depends on our perception, reality would disappear whenever it was not observed by us or others, resp. it

---

[1] G. Berkeley, orig. 1709, (49)

[2] The example of the person born blind can already be found at Molyneux and Locke (J. Locke, 1979, 8, 146)

[3] K. Gibran, The Madman, 2008

would emerge newly out of nonentity every time we perceived it ("creatio ex nihilo").

The question must be allowed if, in the logic of empiricist reasoning, we here do not have the case of a "petitio principii" (subreption of the evidence base). Because, on the one hand, empiricists affirm that we have to take as a basis the sensory perception in order to gain cognition, on the other hand, shortly after, it is demonstrated that just this experience is contradictory and thereby the dissolution of the material world induced.

Empiricism, however, should be credited with the fact that this result at the beginning was by no means intended and, unlike in subjectivism, was not set out at the starting point. The conclusions rather result from the endeavour to take the data from the environment as representative and to see how far they can give us certainty.

While George Berkeley already paved the way for the idea that material things dissolve in reality, David Hume later on takes up this thought and drives it to its logical consequence, i. e. the dissolution of substance but also of identity in general. For, if we are not able to authenticate things, substances, persons, by our sensory perception, not only the outer world but also we ourselves end in dissolution.

If we adhere strictly to our perceptions we also, after all, cannot talk about ourselves as temporally stable substance with an identity, but rather are we exposed to a continuous flood of changing sensory impressions which, from simple ideas, we "assemble" to the complex idea of our identity. This is one of the reasons why Hume's epistemology has been called a "phantasmagoria".

Hume thereby already anticipates many thoughts of system theory, like the process-oriented nature and entelechy of living systems as they are equally expressed in the individual scientific disciplines, as we have seen.

Another philosopher, so to speak the Doyen of all philosophers, the Greek Socrates, has to be seen as innovator of system theory, too. Unlike the English empiricists of the 18th century, he was one of the first to conceptualize systemic thinking even though he did not yet think it out methodically.

Socrates is especially interesting as regards system theory because with reference to its didactical and pedagogical aspects, he conceived in his "Maieutics" (Greek: midwives art) already many ideas that we can use today in personnel management, pedagogy or in therapeutical consulting.

Socrates (469-399 BC)

## "I know that I know nothing!"

The Socratic method of 'maieutics' got its name because of the fact that Socrates' mother was a midwife. Also, the Socratic method with its questioning technique brings only to life in the interviewee the knowledge that was beforehand already sticking in him, thus comparable to a midwife who helps bring to life a child. Socrates' statement "I know that I know nothing!" – meanwhile well-known by everybody – expresses Socrates' endeavour, when questioning Athenian citizens on the market square on most varied issues, to avoid exposing their possible ignorance. He did not want to snub them while he himself appeared to know all the answers.

He rather tried to find out with his questioning technique if the interviewees disposed of any knowledge. As most of the time, it turns out that the interviewees do not have the knowledge that they believe to have, the interrogation ends up in a state of puzzlement, called "aporia". Socrates has the advantage over the interviewees that he at least knows about not having any knowledge of the examined object, a fact which, after all, is to be rated like knowledge (the so-called Socratic irony).

Later on, when discussing systemic counselling as suggested by for instance Steve de Shazer, we will once again come across the pedagogical method of Socrates, described by Aristotle as follows:

### "Socrates only asked questions, but he did not reply."[1]

Socrates asks questions, examines the answers and abstains himself from any statements.[2]

In the further pedagogical and didactical adaptation, the Socratic method of Maieutics leads to a comprehension of teaching where the teacher does not present to the pupils the finished conclusions, but he guides the pupils by questions in such a way that they can gain the conclusions by own insight.[3]

Research was not able to clarify if Socrates did dispose of knowledge but pretended ignorance as pedagogical trick or if, indeed, he himself did

---

[1] Aristotle, 1922, 66, 183 b, own translation
[2] Cp. G. Martin, 1967, 101, own translation
[3] Cp. G. Martin, 1967, 129, own translation

not know either. If one assumes that the latter is correct[1], one has to ask, though, how precise questions can be asked without having defined beforehand one's own position, resp. assumption.

Also, it remains doubtful how Socrates was able to examine the answers of the interviewees without having himself an examining position, from the basis of which a statement could be made.

By the way, this view was neither shared by his follower Platon, nor by Aristotle or Socrates himself. Platon calls him not to be surpassed in comprehension, Aristotle praises his methodical knowledge and Socrates defends himself during his plea in the court – that will finally sentence him to death – as the wisest of all Greeks.[2]

Socrates' maieutic method has had a special influence on pedagogy, for example on the educational concept of the Swiss developmental psychologist Jean Piaget.

At this point, we have now arrived at the systemic concepts as they have established themselves in pedagogy, didactics, counselling and therapy.

### 7.1.5 System Theory, Pedagogy and Counselling

> *"To my children I explained incredibly little;*
> *I taught them neither ethics nor religion; but when*
> *they were quiet…I asked them: will you not become*
> *more reasonable and well-behaved if you are like this,*
> *instead of making noise?"*
> *Pestalozzi[3]*

#### Piaget (1896-1980)

Jean Piaget, in his psychological research on children, again and again pointed out that children do not want to take over fixed rules in the course of their maturation process, but that they want to and also should discover their way by own efforts and personal experiences, provided society expects from this new generation not only the imitation

---

[1]  G. Martin, for example, argues for this perception: Ibid., 1967, 129

[2]  Cp. Platon, Phaidon, 1988, Volume II, 133 (118St.), Aristoteles, Metaphysik, 1995, 19 (987b) and 274 (1078b), Platon, Apologie, Volume I, 32f. (23St.)

[3]  J. H. Pestalozzi, 1927, X III, 15, own translation

of the old, but rather a better world that is to be enriched by this new generation.[1] To reach this, however, it becomes apparent

> "...that its success essentially depends on the role of the teachers. Their most important task consists in creating an arrangement of problems to be studied, and to provide ways in which the problems may actively be dealt with, as well as to keep themselves available in the background as a resource and, if need be, to help the children's attempts for solution into the right direction by asking maieutic questions in the tradition of Socrates."[2]

Piaget, because of his developmental psychological observations, stands in for a sort of epistemological constructivism that only in the process of growth makes emerge the psychic structure in its entelechy. Cognition is being built up from the earliest days of life especially by the active and constructive role of the individual subject.[3]

> "In the general opinion, the outside world is completely separated from the subject although it includes the body of the subject...Indeed, all development stages, especially the sensorimotor and prelingual stages of cognitive adaptation and intelligence are contradictory to this passive understanding of the act of cognition...these structures are not the result of a construction; they do not exist in the objects because they depend on actions, neither do they exist in the subject because it still has to learn to coordinate its actions (which, apart from the reflexes or instincts, in general are not hereditarily fixed)."[4]

This entelechy in child development accordingly leads to the conviction in practice that the pace of learning must be individually measured:

> "For every single subject there is an ideal speed for the transition from one stage to the following, i.e. the stability and even the fruitfulness of a new organization (or restructuring) depends on linkings that do not become apparent immediately but cannot be deferred for too long either because otherwise they would lose their ability to internal linkings."[5]

---

[1] Cp. J. Piaget, 1999, 140
[2] J. Piaget, 1999, 139f., own translation
[3] R. Fatke, 2003, 13
[4] J. Piaget, 2003, 43f., 45, own translation
[5] J. Piaget, 2003, 71, own translation

Piaget points out that his view is being influenced by the biological self-regulation processes:

> "If, on the contrary, we explain maintenance rather with operations and assume that quantities require a complex construction and not only an act of perception, we de facto move from empiricism towards constructivism which is another form of epistemology; moreover, this approach is much closer to current biological trends which emphasize the necessity of constructive self-regulation...The synthesis of the concepts of structure and genesis that determines psychogenetic research finds its justification in the biological concepts of self-regulation and organization and approaches an epistemological constructivism...[1]

As we have seen in the statements referring to the English empiricism, Piaget is wrong here as far as the epistemological classification of empiricism and constructivism is concerned. What is essential, however, is that his basic assumptions are consistent with them. The individual period of time that Piaget allows individuals for their learning processes corresponds to the individual concessions that another humanist, the founder indeed of our modern institutionalized education, Wilhelm von Humboldt, in general grants the students.

## Humboldt (1767-1835)

Wilhelm von Humboldt pleads for education for its own sake, as individual education of all man and not as a purpose-full process that already anticipates and determines (in the sense of a formal training) the goals of education:

> "Therefore, university instruction does not have any limit towards its end and for the students, strictly speaking, a characteristic for maturity is not to be determined. If, how long and in what manner he, once in possession of proficient school knowledge, still continues to need verbal direction? It only depends on the subject. Listening to lectures happens only coincidentally; what is really the essentially necessary is that the young man, between instruction years and admission into life, spends a number of years exclusively with scientific reflection at a place that brings together a lot of people, teachers and learners."[2]

---

[1] J. Piaget, 2003, 125, 129, own translation
[2] W. v. Humboldt, 1988, Gesammelte Schriften, XIII, 261f., own translation

*Systemic Counselling*

A further branch of systemically oriented didactics can be found in the field of systemic counselling with a smooth transition to systemic therapy. Some contents of systemic counselling have already been discussed in the chapter on coaching. Systemic counselling is especially interesting in our context because it constitutes a concrete practical utilization of systemic fundamentals and therefore, like any theory applied in practical experience, has to prove its direct usefulness and success.

Especially if one compares the duration of treatment of systemic solution-focused brief therapy with the classical psychotherapy it becomes evident that here, with the focus on future and solution orientation, amazingly effective achievements can be observed. Essential in our context, however, is the method that was taken over from system theory and was then subject to further development. We here feel reminded of the statements concerning the maieutic questioning techniques by Socrates:

> "The therapist [of the Solution Focused Therapy SFT] is expert for the questioning technique, the client is expert with regards to developing solutions concerning the content. This requires complete reservation by the therapist. Even if he thinks to know better what is good for the client he has to rely on the belief that the client is already in possession of all resources needed, but that only at the moment they are not accessible to him…In order to keep back his own opinion up to such a degree, for the therapist it is helpful to adopt an attitude of not knowing and not evaluating…As the therapist does not give the client any indication referring to the problem, the process of change emanates from the client."[1]

The psychotherapist Insa Sparrer has further developed this approach in "Therapy without Audible Answers". Here, it is sufficient if the therapist asks questions to the clients and the clients indicate when they have answered the question for themselves. The therapist does not have to know the content of the answer; he relies on the competence of the client to solve the problem himself.[2]

---

[1] I. Sparrer, 2006, 35f., own translation; Cp. A.v. Schlippe, 2007
[2] Cp. I. Sparrer, 2006, 2007

## 7.1.6 System Theory and Sociology

There are a number of systemic adaptations to sociological theorems that would exceed the frame of our subject and that to some extent are not relevant to us either. Essentially, the statements of constructivists, sociologists and communication experts – whom, to simplify things, we mention in one context – refer to the systemic fundamentals that we have already mentioned within the different interdisciplinary contexts. We therefore do not want to enter into detailed discussions with the statements of for instance E. v. Glaserfeld, H. v. Förster, P. Watzlawick or N. Luhmann.[1]

We would, however, like to mention one aspect that kept being emphasized by sociologists and which refers to the systemic character of social systems. For instance the American sociologist Talcott Parsons (1902-1979) forms the idea to compare social systems with complex systems, similar to Frederic Vester (see Chapter 7.1.1) with his design of networked system theory:

> "Our position is sharply in disagreement: it derives particularly from Durkheim's statement that society – and other social systems – is a "reality *sui generis.*"
>
> ...We define society as the type of a social system, the characteristic of which is a maximum of selfsufficiency in relation to its environment, including other systems. Perfect selfsufficiency, however, would be incompatible with the status of the society as an action subsystem. Every society depends as far as its maintenance as system is concerned on the inputs from the exchange with systems from its environment. Selfsufficiency in relation to the environment therefore means stability of the exchange relations and the ability to control exchange operations in the interest of a good functioning of the society. This control may consist in the ability to deal with disturbances or to anticipate them, or in the ability to influence the conditions of environment favourably."[2]

---

[1] Cp. z. B. Glasersfeld/Foerster/Watzlawick/Hejl/Schmidt, Einführung in den Konstruktivismus oder Waqtzlawick, Wie wirklich ist die Wirklichkeit?

[2] T. Parsons, 2003, 15, 17, own translation

## 7.1.7 System Theory and Management

There have been repeated efforts to integrate systemic approaches into management theory, however, as far as we know there is only little systematic scientific work that would allow statements concerning the transferability to management theories. There is, though, some very interesting pioneer work done. Fritjof Capra and the Management Consultants Roswitha Königswieser and Christian Lutz, for example, have quite early started to integrate systemic elements into consultancy work.

As aspects that would characterize such a systemic-evolutionary management they mention for instance 1) "from the part to the whole", 2) "from objects to relations", 3) "from structures to processes", and finally 4) "from objectivity to the construction of reality".[1]

The new systemic view, so they say, comprises a paradigm shift away from the classical understanding of the role of the executive as "man of action", away from a "hard" thinking as well as from a "masculine" principle based on objectivity and causality. The systemic view of the world would consist of "networking", the executive would be understood as "developer" and "gardener" and a change to "soft" thinking would be taking place. This would be characterized on the one hand by "self-organization", "subjectivity" and process-orientation,[2] but also by intuition instead of rationality, synthesis instead of analysis, holistic approach instead of reduction as well as cooperation instead of competition.[3] Capra took the approach even further in applying the theory of living systems on human organizations.[4]

The authors mention how much resistance with regard to this new paradigm they used to encounter in the top management offices despite their long-lasting consulting experience. Top management became afraid to lose power and control to the same extent as at the base the emergence of self-developing processes, personal responsibility and "autonomous", entrepreneurially acting working teams with short decision-making processes took place.[5]

---

[1] F. Capra/A. Exner/R. Königswieser, Veränderung im Management – Management der Veränderung, 1992, 113

[2] R. Königswieser, Widerstände gegen systemische Unternehmensführung, 1992, 2

[3] Ibid., 120

[4] F. Capra, 2002, 100f.

[5] C. Lutz, Unternehmensführung im Zeitalter der Kommunikation, 1992, 143

Yet, so their experience, by no means systemic thinking replaces the decisions of management, on the contrary, it ends up in a strengthening of company functions like business policy, communication as well as personnel and organizational development.[1]

By the classical power structures in enterprises the self-direction potential would be destroyed and thereby also the creative resources of organizational subsystems which for crisis management had a high value. Therefore, this would weaken enterprises.[2]

Modern leadership credo, today, would orientate itself more and more on the employees themselves:

> "Leading means to bring their best out of people. For this, one must help them to do it themselves. This works if people are encouraged to develop their own potential as much as they can do it themselves..."[3]

This would also include to admit the critical faculties of employees and even to encourage them.

*"Something that does not offer resistance, one cannot lean on".*

*Charles de Gaulles*

The ability to self-direction, but also the drive for it, should precisely not be considered as an attitude opposed to company interests. The English economic philosopher Charles Handy goes so far as to affirm that progress depends on unreasonable people because reasonable people would adapt themselves to the world while unreasonable ones would adapt the world to their own ideas.[4]

> "Entrepreneurial processes of change therefore are being pushed on by unreasonable people and thus above all by properly managed emotions and intuitions."[5]

---

[1] F. Capra/A. Exner/R. Königswieser, Veränderung im Management – Management der Veränderung, 1992, 112

[2] M. Lueger, Macht und Herrschaft in Organisationen, 1992, 177

[3] H. H. Hinterhuber, 2007, 209, own translation

[4] Handy, C., The Age of Unreason. London, 1999, 4

[5] H. H. Hinterhuber, 2007, 40, own translation

In Chapter 5 on Theories of Leadership we had already mentioned that decisions necessarily are being made by emotions and not by pure rationality – this meaning in the language of system theory, "soft", "networked", "circular" thinking. The use of these attributes, however, should by no means give raise to any false connotations in the direction of a "cuddle management".

Even in military thinking relevant aspects can be found. For example, the Prussian Field Marshal Helmuth von Moltke (1800-1891) designed directives instead of orders and instructions because he considered initiative acting as so important that for it he was even prepared to accept divergences from his action plans. The method of directives thus led to the "individualization of leadership". H.H. Hinterhuber therefore describes him in his leadership method "as more progressive than many enterprises of our time".[1]

> "Moltke trained the non-commissioned officers to see their own, particular problems and possibilities as well as their possible solutions in the bigger frame of the whole general issue.[2]

> "It is obvious that for this, theoretical knowledge does not suffice, but that here the characteristics of the intellect as well as those of the personality are expressed in their free, practical, in their artistic creativity …".[3]

## Malik (*1944)

When looking at the statements of the Austrian economist Fredmund Malik, inter alia founder of the Management Zentrum St. Gallen, concerning the range of topics on leadership, here also the tendency can be observed to increasingly understand personnel leadership individually, in the sense of self-direction:

> "Ultimately, development can only come from people themselves, just as they can only change themselves…Almost anything that has to do with the development of people has to happen individually."[4]

---

[1] H.H. Hinterhuber, 2007, 126 et seq.

[2] H. Rosinski, Die deutsche Armee, Düsseldorf, 1970, 125, own translation

[3] H. v. Moltke, Militärische Werke. Ed. Vom Großen Generalstab. 13Bd., Berlin, 1892, 170, own translation

[4] F. Malik, 2001, 248, own translation

Fredmund Malik points out that not so much the selection of executives should be in the focus but rather their education. Accordingly, leadership should be understood as a profession like any other profession.[1] A formal training like it is common in disciplines like medicine, architecture or engineering still has to win recognition in management[2]:

> "It attracts attention that only few executives have a systematic training in management...Basically, there are still only two organizations that prepare their future executives really systematically for their leadership tasks in a narrower sense and not only for their function and to-the-purpose tasks: the army and the church."[3]

Malik's statements that are generally very practically-oriented, besides an adequate management training that understands management as profession, call for two additional qualifications on the part of potential executives: to serve as a role model and to dispose of integrity as regards their character.[4] Malik here intentionally leaves open the scientific justification as well as more detailed explanations. What is important for him is functionality and usefulness. Accordingly, for him, management theory is not to be understood as science:

> "I do not belief management itself to be a science but...a practical experience...the goals of science and of management are completely different ones...Science aims at knowledge, management at utility. Science orients itself on truth, management on efficiency...Theory asks: Is it true? Management asks: Does it work?...Management gets the character of a discipline...for the reason that it is an interface between art, science and common sense.[5]

Much as he gives consideration to the active, self-determined and individualized view of man and thereby to leadership strategy, Malik's focus still remains on the executive, his education and his behaviour. He de-

---

[1]  F. Malik, 2001, 45
[2]  F. Malik, 2001, 385
[3]  F. Malik, 2001, 55, own translation
[4]  F. Malik, 256
[5]  F. Malik, 2001, 388, 390, own translation

serves the credit to have claimed professionalization in management education and by this claim to have formulated new standards of quality for executives as well as their management performance.

When talking about Systemic Leadership (a term that actually has not yet established itself in this form), the primacy would have to be seen with the employee. A paradigm change takes place from the executive that classically has been in the focus of all leadership theories, now shifting toward the employee and his needs, abilities and possibilities.

Before examining what implications the design of a Systemic Leadership could have on the executive and his leadership theory, we should recapitulate what insights we can gain by the systemic approach in the various disciplines.

## 7.2 Summary

We now have explored in what form system theory – if one can speak at all of a holistic theorem – has found its expression in the different disciplines. Similar thoughts in most different disciplines have been formulated at different times and independent from each other.

It was by no means our task to present system theory as dominant explanatory model or to maintain the necessity of the alleged ideas compared to other paradigms. What we wanted is to show the central theme that can be observed across time and across the different disciplines by presenting selected examples.

And this should not be understood as an end in itself. If we want to give consideration to the question in what way in business sciences, in the section human resources management, and here again in the subsection personnel management, system theory can be understood and applied, we are moving in far bigger surroundings.

In order to cover the questions referring to how to deal with people, their communication among each other, the way they can be motivated to good performance or how personnel management in organizations ought to be carried out, it will not suffice to limit oneself to considerations on purely economic or human sciences.

On the contrary, we should ask ourselves how living and complex systems function and act in general and what principles of law are working in nature. Here, our knowledge of physics, biology, and evolutionary theory may be useful in order to prevent us from developing purely ideal or utopian thoughts.

On the other hand, it may also be useful to examine carefully these results and findings in order to be able to effectively respond to ideological prejudices and to be open for creative thinking and behaviour patterns that, otherwise, may not be paid attention to.

In the following we will give a short résumé on some core statements that may be concluded from the results of the mentioned discipline branches for the functioning of living systems. Subsequently we will draw our conclusions for Leadership.

## Biology

We have seen that biological and evolutionary systems may only be understood in the context of an integrated whole. Living systems are operationally closed; at the same time they maintain – because of their dependence on metabolic processes – their structural openness (Bertalanffy).

The fact that they are operationally closed has as a consequence that living systems are subject to change because of their inherent organization and their self-contained order. Living systems did not emerge as adaptation to their environment, they equally adapt their environment to themselves (Lovelock). Organisms do not react passively to environmental stimulus as information carrier that releases causal effects but according to their inherent order. Environment only "disturbs" the organism without influencing the operational changes of the organism with regard to their content (Capra).

In evolution, living systems are characterized by the laws of mutation, selection and openness (Eigen). Instead of competition, the strategies successful in evolution are cooperation, networking and co-evolution (Capra/Margulis).

## Physics

Physical cybernetics also shows that complex systems are characterized by their inherent order (Wiener). These inherent orders emerge as dissipative, self-organizational structures amongst disorder (Prigogine/Haken).

Dissipative structures and entropy are not to be considered as contradiction (Gell-Mann). Also, the emission of electromagnetic radiation takes place autonomously according to Planck's quantum jumps.

Processes in nature are not causally describable but only with probabilities; the same causes do not have the same effects. Also, we cannot talk of an objectively existing nature; observer and nature cannot be separated (Heisenberg).

## Chaos Research

Chaos research demonstrates the emergence of autonomous pattern if systems are left to themselves. The same result can be observed in nonlinear mathematics with the formation of attractors (Mandelbrot).

Basically, chaotic systems are describable and therefore are at least theoretically determined (Capra). Especially at the edge of the chaos, complex self-organizational structures are emerging and show precisely there their highest performance and ability to change (Briggs/Peat/ Kauffman).

This self-organization ("order for free" according to Kauffman) takes place even before any selection; accordingly this would mean that the assumption of a gradual evolution on the selection level in the sense of Darwin was wrong (Kauffman/Dawkins).

## Cognition Science

In cognition sciences as well the paradigm of a self-organizational nervous system with own structures formed itself. According to this, brains would not work locally, and neither would they work in the trivial sense of computers or machines (Capra).

Accordingly, our cognition does not focus on an environment that would exist independently from ourselves, but on the contrary, our brain determines the world instead of mirroring it. Organism and environment are operationally closed and therefore they are systems independent from each other. For the nervous system, essential in evolution is survivability and not the representation of the environment (Varela).

This means that there is no survival of the more adapted. We could also survive with an "error" regarding the correct perception of the environment. For the evolutionary survivability, all there is needed is the ability for replication (Maturana/Varela).

## Philosophy

Occidental as well as oriental philosophical systems have been holding the view of subjectivistic ("self-organizatonal") concepts for a long time. If we examine for example the constructs of nominalism and empiricism, our reality is dissipating, and this all the more if we count on the 'certain' perceptions of our sensory experiences. This is demonstrated by mental delusions as well as by our use of collective terms that do not correspond to anything real in the world. Even for our inner world, our identity, evidence as a substance cannot be provided; there just remains a procedural sequence of impressions (Berkeley/Hume). Socrates' maieutics represents a first didactical and pedagogical method to understand man in the systemic context.

## Pedagogy

Developmental psychology supports the view that learning is to be understood as a constructive, active and individual act, especially as far as learning speed is concerned (Piaget), and the claim for it, in the sense of institutional education, should include that its purpose should purely be its own sake (Humboldt).

## Therapy

Systemic thinking, applied in counselling and therapy, shows very good results with regards to future-oriented and result-oriented efficiency. Besides having the faith that the clients, with the help of their own resources, self-organizationally find the solution and activate the ability for the necessary change, the therapist is required to adopt an attitude of Socratic nescience (de Shazer, v. Schlippe, Sparrer).

## Sociology

Sociological theories also have described systemic thinking in the adaptation to societies and their sub-systems as realities of their own (Parsons).

## Management

System theory has already been applied to management- and organizational theories under various definitions and specifications. General descriptions have been given of the systemic manager as network thinker, gardener, developer who is characterized by soft, process-oriented, intuitive and holistic thinking, away from competition, toward cooperation (Capra, Königswieser).

The executive brings out the best in the employees by helping them to do it themselves, by developing their potential. The leadership consists in acknowledging their subjectivity and individuality and in encouraging their critical faculty (Hinterhuber).

Precisely by admitting self-organizational structures, creativity is activated, an attribute urgently needed to solve entrepreneurial crises (Lutz/Lueger).

For successful leadership, personal qualifications are required, however, not sufficient. Leadership has to be professionalized by an instrumental education (Malik).

# Chapter 8

# Systemic Leadership

*"He who wants to lead people should walk behind them."*
*Laotse*

If we use as a stepping stone the results of the statements on system theory from Chapter 7 as an outline on Systemic Leadership, we can deduct six theses that are mainly relevant for our context:

## 8.1 Six Theses

1) Organisms live each in their particularly constructed world as systems existing independently from each other; we cannot assume an environment common to all of them. An adaptation to the environment in the sense of a representation may not offer any advantage for survival.

2) Organisms do not act and react similarly but according to their own inherent order and therefore individually. The application of the same measures to all of them will lead to unpredictable reactions.

3) Not competition, but cooperation and networking are successful strategies in evolution.

4) Organisms organize themselves even amongst disorder.

5) Learning, changing and problem solving happen individually, on one's own activity and constructively, with the help of own resources.

6) The creativity set free by self-organization increases the chances of survival of enterprises.

At this point we can certainly ask ourselves how far some of the theses because of their micro-physical or micro-biological character and scale may be applied and are transferable to the mesocosmos of man. The question, though, remains unanswerable – neither we nor any of the quoted authors have a reply to it.

What is important in this context, however, is that there are no contradictions between the criteria and systems of observance, for example that dissipation and entropy are as well compatible as attractors in chaos or determinism and chaos theory. If, thus, we assume that transferability is admissible, the question now arises what conclusions we have to draw from the six theses with regards to personnel leadership.

## 8.2 Consequences for Leadership

### 8.2.1 From Environment to System, from Manager to Employee

Let us begin with the most evident aspect. While traditional management theories focus on the management strategy and especially on the executive as a person, the systemic approach asks for a paradigm shift toward the person to be guided, the employee. The reasons for it are on the one hand that for the individual consideration of every employee it is not adequate to apply the limited arsenal of management styles, like represented for instance by the Situative Management style of Hersey & Blanchard or the Managerial Grid of Blake & Mouton.

On the other hand, by applying the same method to different employees, the result cannot be predicted if we assume a constructive order of its own for each particular employee and the consequences this has to his driving force of motivation.

Classical leadership models assume that people have to be directed because they are not able to direct themselves. However, we have seen in Lewin's "Iowa" studies concerning leadership in Chapter 5 that for instance under the autocratic management style, the executive's absence has the consequence that employee performance considerably decreases, while under the democratic management style the employee performance remains stable even in the executive's absence.

If, furthermore, we have to assume that direction does not happen informatively, as a stimulus referring to content, but rather as disturbance which keeps the employee from doing what is consistent with his own goals and strives to self-contained deployment, then direction in its real sense cannot happen at all and, indeed, has never happened.

Here we could possibly find the reason for the inefficiency of leadership performance that is being observed everywhere, as well as the lack of methodical training as criticised by F. Malik. The reasons for successful leadership are not clear and this again may have its cause in the fact that we do not know how man and his motivation are to be understood. It does not seem amazing if for instance in the GLOBE study Robert House postulates as result of successful global leadership the aspect "man orientation" before "business orientation", resp. the statement that if the characteristics and behaviour of the directing person do fit with the expectations of the employees as to how they should be directed, this increases significantly the success of leadership. [1]

If motivation is to be understood as own stimulus based on emotion and not on intellectual power, it becomes clear that it cannot be produced by information coming from outside. Knowledge can be communicated, willingness cannot. Therefore, if one can only motivate oneself and if this impetus has to be understood as a personal and emotional one [2], we have to ask ourselves what exactly is the kind of contribution on the part of the executive that makes it possible for the employee to motivate himself to his maximum.

If we take system theory as a base, we do not have to depend on hope for this motivation because, in the sense of self-organization, it is already inherent in man. Therefore, it is not a question of providing a stimulus from outside to make people perform, as stated in Theory X by McGregor, but rather, in the sense of Theory Y, to make possible a willingness to perform that is already existing – and in the sense of system theory, we even would have to say – instead of preventing it.

If, according to all this, within Systemic Leadership, we cannot consider as reasonable the standardization of leadership methods, this does not have to mean a denial with regards to the professionalization of executive education as claimed by F. Malik. A paradigm shift will do.

Instead of the training of executives in various management methods that are then supposed to be applied to the employees without consideration of their individual needs, executives should only be trained in one important technique. This technique is to be understood, in the sense of the maieutic approach, simply as a technique to make competent. By doing this, does the executive not himself change his own role

---

[1] See Chapter 6.5.2
[2] See Chapter 5.1

to that of a consultant and coach of the employee, and does he not make himself redundant as far as "direction" is concerned?

## 8.2.2 Company Objectives and Employee Objectives

While, indeed, direction in the actual sense of system theory does not take place any more – because the employee directs himself on a way which is only known to himself – the power of decision making certainly has to stay with the executive, and also company targets may continue to be broken down to department targets and finally also to individual targets. It would be absurd to see company targets and interests as genuinely opposed to employee targets and interests. Employee interests will never be completely different from company interests, and vice versa company interests will always have to co-orient themselves on employee interests.

Systemic Leadership precisely is a suitable tool to optimize this co-orientation of company performance and employee performance because the individual performance can be increased considerably when a high degree of motivation is reached.

Employee targets that are recognized and admitted in their individual genesis may offer additional creative potential because not only the employees, by following their visions and ideas, will work with maximum motivation but also chances that otherwise the enterprise would possibly not have seen, may find consideration. In practice, the individual targets of employees will not completely be outside the frame of the company targets. It is however realistic to expect that actual department and division priorities may be completed or reorganized, and this will not lead to a weakening but rather to a fortification of the competitiveness of an enterprise.

## 8.2.3 Competition

The idea of competition, in the classical evolutionary understanding, comes from mutual assertiveness and the consequential selection. If however, as explained in Chapter 7, order in self-organized systems is already being produced before any selection has taken place, we perhaps should abandon the view that competition is to be seen as the decisive evolutionary strategy.

If moreover, according to the statements of modern evolutionary biology, precisely not competition, but cooperation as well as networking are successful strategies in evolution, the question arises why in our business world again and again Hobbes' Homo Homini Lupus resp. the Bellum Omnium Contra Omnes[1] preferably receive attention, attitudes which allegedly already characterized the state of nature of man.

To define the nature of man as egoistic, belligerent and being in continuous competitive fight with others, after all, is quite arbitrary because any quantity of arguments may as well be found against this thesis. In our context, however, we are interested above all in the fact that competition in the systemic view is no successful construct for individual nor for company strategies. In addition to the reasons that can be found in evolutionary biology, also from the purely systemic point of view, competition not only is absurd but also impossible.

If we assume the self-organization of living beings that have their own targets inherent within them in accordance with their own order, competition in the sense of comparison of two systems on the basis of a third criterion (tertium comperationis) does not make any sense. Autopoietic systems try to become, in accordance with their entelechy, the 'best' version of themselves, in other words they want to operate following their own inherent order. As this process necessarily is an individual one, two persons cannot really be compared with each other and with this, the idea of competition looses its sense. If competition is understood as the comparison of two persons with the help of an external benchmark, all we will measure is the quantities of a performance, but what we will not capture and therefore not enhance is the different qualities as they find their expression for instance in creative performance.

Thus, in the systemic sense, there cannot be competition between two persons, because apples and oranges cannot be compared. Even with ourselves we cannot enter into competition; all we can do at best is to work on the development of our talents. This, as discussed in the statements on identity[2], however, because of the process-orientation of our

---

[1] Cp. Chapter 5.2

[2] The objection, by the way, that to our own identity we could only find through others which is based on Hegel's thought that affirmation necessarily means always at the same time negation, is not applicable for the same reason that survival would theoretically also be possible with an epistemological error. It is essential that negation takes place, but as little as representation of the outer world is necessary, this negation is determinant as to content. Communication and interaction with others, in the systemic sense, are always perturbing, not instructing.

being, cannot be a comparison by means of a fixed criterion, and therefore, we ourselves cannot be confronted with such a fixed criterion either. Competition, accordingly, does not even make sense as a competition with ourselves.

## 8.2.4 Performance

Accordingly, also the statement that man would only develop his performance potential in an optimal way under competition needs to be verified. Rather the question should be asked if not precisely under competition the ability to perform is not drastically reduced, if we know that ability and willingness to perform exist, before any selection takes place, in the self-organization of all beings and that interactions from the outside only affect as perturbations to this ability to perform.

If we transfer this to practical consequences, it would mean that according to systemic understanding, performance would indeed actively be brought in, however, that a benchmark for intersubjective performance measuring, like it is conceived and practiced for example in the form of a performance-based compensation, would loose its sense. But to the degree that performance-based compensation is precisely adopted as motivation instrument to reach willingness to perform, this may not really be regarded as a loss since this kind of motivation necessity may now cease to be applied.

As far as personnel development is concerned, this new view on the employees, even on today's basis, is well imaginable. But how can we think personnel selection in practice under this paradigm without it becoming a utopia? How is the selection of employees reasonably to be carried out without disposing of any third criteria by the means of which two employees may be measured? Would that not mean to take ad absurdum all personnel selection instruments that up to now have been proving high validity and projection quality as to their suitability diagnosis?

Verification shows that the systemic paradigm, far from replacing the existing suitability diagnosis, rather completes it because targets, development wishes and motivations of potential employees have a tendency to attract more attention and, therefore, a shift of the assessment criteria from ability to willingness takes place.

Let us take a look at personnel development. If the performance of employees will not be compared any more between each other, how else can performance be measured? A change might be appropriate away from the comparison of the performance of several employees toward a reconciliation of specific positional and functional characteristics in the enterprise with the qualifications and motivations of the employees. But would that not produce again an external standard of comparison through the back-door that indirectly compares the employee by means of the position profile as criterion?

A second thought on the systemic paradigm for organizational development will disclose that merely matching the employee qualification with company profiles definitely would be an inadequate approach. The requirement would rather be that the functional and positional profiles defined on the side of the company leave the necessary leeway so that they can be filled individually by the qualification and motivation of the employees that fill the job and thus individual career development paths can be defined. But would that not mean that an enterprise makes itself dependent on the employees and their individual targets?

In the sense of co-evolution, enterprises and employees as well as environment and system have always been mutually depending on each other, anyway. The actually usual, rather one-sidedly forced adaptation of the employees to the company culture does not change anything on this fact, because also today already we have to admit that it is no-one else but the employees themselves with all their individuality that form the company culture as a whole. With the idea of co-evolution in the back of one's mind, it is therefore by all means insured that employee motivation and interests can be included effectively into the company interests.

When coming to the question of a concrete management technique within Systemic Leadership, especially Feedback as performance management instrument seems appropriate, as described in Chapter 2. Feedback as cybernetic feedback loop that makes it possible for self-organized systems to change their self-structuredness in the sense of an active and volitional learning process which, as we have seen, cannot be thought otherwise than autonomous and without any directional reaction on feedback contents. Nevertheless, performance here can be measured for instance in a 360° assessment. It will then primarily not be used to compare different performances but it will focus on the individual possibility to improve one's own performance.

Also, we may ask ourselves if the systemic approach in personnel leadership, as we have explained it, can be applied to all employees or – to use for instance the nomenclature of Hersey & Blanchard – if this requires a certain "level of maturity" on the part of the employee and therefore would be applicable only to a few highly qualified persons.

*"The higher its type, always the seldomer*
*doth a thing succeed."*

Friedrich Nietzsche[1]

If we examine the system theory of living organisms, a differentiation concerning the entelechy of living beings cannot be made as regards quality, i.e. their way of operation. But could not a differentiation be made between higher and lesser developed living beings and thereby an allocation in quantitative degrees of development?

We have seen that the paradigm of a selective, gradual adaptation cannot be maintained – even vis-à-vis ourselves, we would not be able to apply degrees on our ontogenetic maturity with the help of an individual benchmark. If evolution is not understood teleologically, then this cannot be a criterion for ontogenesis either.

We therefore cannot speak of different degrees of maturity because they would presume a quantitative scale of comparison for our maturity. In Systemic Leadership, though, this does not mean any disadvantage because the danger to confront and guide employees with too high expectations as to their maturity simply does not exist. Employees, by their willingness and their targets, define themselves how they want to be "guided".

If one reflects on these thoughts in a concrete and practical way, the question may arise how Systemic Leadership could change the culture of a whole organization resp. what kind of environment around an enterprise Systemic Leadership would require. Teams on their own responsibility could decide on successors to fill the job, teams would select themselves their executives, employees would define themselves and initiatively their targets, etc. What becomes apparent here is a big field of future fruitful research projects that is waiting to be farmed, in order to turn the outlined approaches into entrepreneurial management practice.

Many more examples could be quoted that confirm systemic approaches as successful strategy. We would for instance like to mention mediation which is so successful precisely because the disputing parties

---

[1]  F. Nietzsche, Thus Spoke Zarathustra, The Higher Man

reach a solution by themselves that according to all juridical experiences proves to be much more stable than forced solutions of a third party from the outside.[1] Or let us take the actual results of pedagogical research showing that students learn easier if they can acquire the subject matter autonomously. This corresponds to a self-organizational kind of learning because it can take place according to the own inherent structure, while the classical method of a monologue on the part of the teacher shows the worst learning results.[2]

## 8.2.5 Man as an Artist

Furthermore, we may examine areas of art, referring to J. Beuys statement of every man being an artist and pointing out that self-organization, autonomy and creativity in human work emerge precisely by blasting conventional patterns, so to speak by designing a biological blueprint of mutation.

We would like to mention the development of the electric guitar which started in the 1920s with the purpose of making the guitar in an orchestra more assertive and turn up the sound. While the play of the classical guitar had been established as training since a long time and admitted, like is the case with all classical instruments, only one correct technique that had to be acquired in curricular studies, there was not yet any presetting for the big scope of different techniques that then developed in the world of the electric guitar.

Contrary to the classical guitar that had not continued to develop its technique nor its artistic level, artists sprang up like mushrooms that on the electric field developed new possibilities of expression and completely new techniques. This creative abundance would not have emerged if the way to see the instrument and the art as a whole would have been preset already in an institutionalized manner, instead of having been left to the creative freedom of the particular artist.

Thus, we today have artists like for instance Edward Van Halen or Stanley Jordan who on the guitar have adapted completely new techniques, like for instance "tapping" derived from piano playing. They thereby have enriched our musical world in a way that, in the sense of a competitive comparison, comparing artists only by means of a third crite-

---

[1] Cp. Haft/v. Schlieffen, 2008
[2] P. R.-J. Simons, 1992, 251-264

rion – in this case the orthodox, already known way of playing the guitar –never could have happened (and especially not within such a short time).

> *"...I never took lessons, so I didn't know there were rules;*
> *I just knew what I liked and wanted to feel and hear.*
> *This also had a major impact on the way I play,*
> *doing things on the guitar that weren't written*
> *in any books."*
>
> Edward Van Halen [1]

Art and creativity always had to be understood in a systemic context, with the meaning of attributes like active, autonomous, self-organizational, individual, creativity coming out of oneself. In this sense, we have to confirm Beuys' statement of every man being an artist – a master in the art of living and maybe an expert in the art of survival, anyway. When dealing with people, therefore, especially in personnel management, we should take care to treat employees accordingly.

To comprehend people within the mentioned systemic aspects and to "lead" them according to Systemic Leadership offers many chances. We have to admit not only new approaches in personnel and organizational development. System Theory gives us challenges that reach up to our epistemological convictions. This may be no consolation to our metaphysical mourning for our lost reality, even if we realize that our lost realism was nothing but metaphysics for idealism.

> *"...much did I love the world, and the world loved me,*
> *For all my smiles were upon her lips, and*
> *all her tears were in my eyes.*
> *Yet there was between us a gulf of silence*
> *Which she would not abridge*
> *And I could not overstep."*
>
> K. Gibran [2]

---

[1] Guitar World, Vol. 30, No. 2, February 2009, 68
[2] K. Gibran, The Garden of the Prophet, 1998

# Bibliography

*Achouri, C.,* Paradoxale Aspekte empiristischer Ethik. München, Akademischer Verlag, 1998

*Achouri, C.,* Der Zusammenhang von Systemtheorie und sokratischer Maieutik. Information Philosophie. Lörrach, 2001

*Achouri, C.,* Zeit und Identität. Eine philosophische Meditation. Würzburg, Königshausen und Neumann, 2004

*Aristoteles,* Metaphysik IX, 8, Hamburg, Meiner, 1991

*Aristoteles.* Sophistische Widerlegungen (Organon VI). Hamburg, Meiner, 1922

*Bales, R.F., Slater, P.E.,* Role differentiation in small decision making groups, in: Gibb, C. (Ed.), Leadership. Harmondsworth, 1969

*Bass, B.M.,* Does the transactional-transformational leadership paradigm transcend organizational and national boundaries? In: American Psychologist, 52(2), 130-139, 1997

*Bateson, G.,* Steps to an Ecology of Mind. Chicago, The University of Chicago Press, 1972

*Bau Michael, Wilkesmann Uwe* (Hrg.), Human Resource Management – Vom Stiefkind zum strategischen Partner. Reihe: Wirtschaft: Forschung und Wissenschaft, Münster, LIT, Bd. 17, 2006

*Baumer, T.,* Handbuch interkulturelle Kompetenz, Band 1. Zürich, Orell Füssli, 2002

*Baumer, T.,* Handbuch interkulturelle Kompetenz, Band 2. Zürich, Orell Füssli, 2004

*Berger, Peter L./Luckmann, Thomas,* Die gesellschaftliche Konstruktion der Wirklichkeit. Frankfurt, Fischer, 1989

*Bergemann, N., Sourisseaux, A.L.J.,* Interkulturelles Management. Berlin, Springer, 2003

*Berkeley, G.,* An Essay towards a new Theory of Vision. Harvard Press, 2006 (orig. 1709)

*Berne, E.,* Die Transaktionsanalyse in der Psychotherapie. Paderborn, 2006

*Berne, E.,* Grundlagen der Gruppenbehandlung. Paderborn, 2005

*Bertalanffy, Ludwig von:* General System Theory. Foundations, Development, Applications. New York, George Braziller, Inc., 1969

*BDA Bundesvereinigung der Deutschen Arbeitgeberverbände*, Demographie und gesellschaftlicher Wandel. Band 44, 2004

*Blake, R. R.*, Interview with Robert Blake. Healthcare Forum Journal, July-August 1992, Vol. 35, #4, International Copyright 1992, Joe Flower, All Rights Reserved

*Blake, R. R., Mouton, J. S.*, The managerial grid. Houston, 1964

*Blake R. R., Mouton, J. S.*, Verhaltenspsychologie im Betrieb. Düsseldorf, Econ, 1980

*Block Richard J., Yuker Harold E.*, Ich sehe was, was Du nicht siehst. 250 optische Täuschungen und visuelle Illusionen. München, Goldmann, 1996

*Borsche, Tilman*: Wilhelm v. Humboldt. München, Beck, 1990.

*Börnecke, Dirk* (Ed.), Basiswissen für Führungskräfte. Erlangen, Publicis, 2007

*Briggs, J., Peat, F. D.*, Turbulent Mirror. An illustrated Guide to Chaos Theory and the Science of Wholeness. New York, Harper & Row, 1989

*Brodbeck, F. C.*, Die Suche nach universellen Führungsstandards, in: Wirtschaftspsychologie aktuell, 1/2008

*Brodbeck, F. C., Frese, M., Javidan, M.*, Leadership made in Germany, Low on compassion, high on performance. Academy of Management Executive, 16, (1), 16-29

*Bryman, A.*, Charisma and Leadership in Organizations. London, Sage, 1992

*Buck, H, Kistler, E., Mendius, H. G.*, Demographischer Wandel in der Arbeitswelt – Chancen für eine innovative Arbeitsgestaltung. Broschürenreihe "Demographie und Erwerbsarbeit". Stuttgart, 2002

*Bühler, C.*: Theoretical observations about Life's Basic Tendencies. American Journal for Psychotherapy, 13, 1959 (561-581)

*Capra, F.*, The Web Of Life. A new Scientific Understanding of Living Systems. Anchorbooks, 1996

*Capra, F.*, The Hidden Connections. A Science for Sustainable Living. First Anchor Books Edition, 2002

*Capra, F.*, The Tao of Physics: An Exploration of the Parallels between Modern Physics and Eastern Mysticism. Shambhala, 2000

*Capra, F., Exner, A., Königswieser, R.*, Veränderung im Management-Management der Veränderung, in: Königswieser, R./Lutz, C. (Ed.), Das systemisch evolutionäre Management. Wien, Orac, 1992

*Cohn, R. C.*, Von der Psychoanalyse zur Themenzentrierten Interaktion. Stuttgart, Klett-Cotta, 1975

*Comelli, G., Rosenstiel, L. v.*, Führung durch Motivation. Mitarbeiter für Organisationsziele gewinnen. München, Vahlen, 2001

*Daum, J. W.*, Two measures of R.O.I. on intervention-fact or fantasy? In: Cascio, W. F.: Managing human resources: Productivity, Quality of Life, Profits, 1992

*Darwin, C.*, On the Origin of Species. Dover Pubn. Inc., 2006

*Das Tibetanische Totenbuch*. Ein Weisheitsbuch der Menschheit. Artemis & Winkler, Düsseldorf, Patmos, 2003

*Dawkins, R.*, The Blind Watchmaker: Why the evidence of evolution reveals a universe without design. New York, 1987

*Dawkins, R.*, The Selfish Gene. Oxford University Press, 1989

*Dawkins, R.*, The Ancestor's Tale. A Pilgrimage to the Dawn of Evolution. Boston, Mariner Books, 2005

*Deutsche Gesellschaft für Personalführung* (Ed.): Personalcontrolling in der Praxis. Schäffer-Poeschel, 2001

*DuBois, P. H.*, A history of psychological testing. Boston, Allyn & Bacon, 1970

*Eibl-Eibesfeldt, I.*, Der vorprogrammierte Mensch. Kiel, Orion-Heimreiter, 1985

*Eigen, M.*, Stufen zum Leben. Die frühe Evolution im Visier der Molekularbiologie. München, Piper, 1987

*Eigen, M., Winkler, R.*, Das Spiel. Naturgesetze steuern den Zufall. München, Piper, 1996

*Epiktet*, Handbüchlein der Moral und Unterredungen, Stuttgart, Kröner, 1984

*Erpenbeck, J., Rosenstiel, L. v.* (Ed.), Handbuch Kompetenzmessung. Stuttgart, 2003

*Evans-Wentz, W. Y. (Ed.)*, The Tibetan Book of the Dead, Oxford University Press, 1960

*Fatke, R.*, Einführung, in: J. Piaget, Meine Theorie der geistigen Entwicklung. Weinheim, Beltz, 2003

*Fischer, Roger, Ury, William, Patton, Bruce,* Das Harvard Konzept. Der Klassiker der Verhandlungstechnik. Campus, 2003.

*Fleischmann, E. A., Harris, E. F., Burtt, H. E.,* Leadership and supervision in industry. Columbus, 1955

*Forrester, J. W.*, Der teuflische Regelkreis. Stuttgart, dva, 1971

*Fromm, E.*, Anatomie der menschlichen Destruktivität (1973). Hamburg, Rowohlt, 1991

*Fromm, E.*, Haben oder Sein. Die seelischen Grundlagen einer neuen Gesellschaft. München, dtv, 1987

*Fuchs, Johann,* Demographische Alterung und Arbeitskräftepotential. IAB – Colloquium "Praxis trifft Wissenschaft", Eine Frage des Alters, Herausforderungen für eine zukunftsorientierte Beschäftigungspolitik. Lauf, 2003

*Gagné, R.M., Fleischmann, E.A.,* Psychology and human performance, New York, 1959

*Gell-Mann, M.,* The Quark and the Jaguar. Adventures in the Simple and the Complex. New York, W. H. Freeman and Company, 1994

*Gesteland, R.R., Global* Business Behaviour. Zürich, Orell Füssli, 1998

*Gibran, K.,* The Madman. Classic Books Library, 2008

*Gibran, K.,* The Garden of the Prophet. Penguin, 1998

*Haft, F., Schlieffen, K. v.* (Ed.), Handbuch der Mediation. München, Beck Juristischer Verlag, 2008

*Hagehülsmann, H.,* Beratung zu professionellem Wachstum. Die Kunst transaktionsanalytischer Beratung. Paderborn, 2007

*Hagehülsmann, Ute & Heinrich,* Der Mensch im Spannungsfeld seiner Organisation. Transaktionsanalyse in Managementtraining, Coaching, Team- und Personalentwicklung. Paderborn, Junfermann, 1998

*Hare, R.M.,* Wollen: Einige Fallen, in: Analytische Handlungsphilosophie, Bd.1. Ed.: G. Meggle, Frankfurt am Main, 1985

*Heisenberg, W.,* Quantentheorie und Physik. Stuttgart, Reclam, 2006

*Hell, B., Boramir, I., Schaar, H., Schuler, H.,* Interne Personalauswahl und Personalentwicklung in deutschen Unternehmen. In: Wirtschaftspsychologie 1-2006, 8. Jahrgang. Lengerich, Pabst Science.

*Hentze, J., Brose, P.,* Personalführungslehre. Grundlagen, Führungsstile, Funktionen und Theorien der Führung. Ein Lehrbuch für Studenten und Praktiker. UTB, Stuttgart, 1986

*Herbrand, F.,* Fit für fremde Kulturen, Bern, Haupt, 2002

*Hersey, P, Blanchard, K.,* Management of organizational behaviour: Utilizing human resources. Englewood Cliffs, NJ, 1987

*Herzberg, F.,* Work and Nature of Man. London, Crosby Lockwood Staples, 1966

*Hinterhuber, H.,* Leadership. Strategisches Denken systematisch schulen von Sokrates bis heute. Frankfurt am Main, Frankfurter Allgemeine Buch, 2007

*Hobbes, T.,* Leviathan. Cambridge University Press, 1996

*Hoffmann, D.,* Max Planck, Die Entstehung der modernen Physik. München, C.H. Beck, 2008-12-10

*Hofstede, G., Culture's* Consequences. CA, Sage, 1984

*Hofstede, G.,* Lokales Denken, Globales Handeln. München, dtv, 2006

*Hossiep, R., Paschen, M., Mühlhaus, O.,* Persönlichkeitstests im Personalmanagement. Grundlagen, Instrumente und Anwendungen. Göttingen, 1999

*House, R. J., Hanges, P. J., Javidan, M., Dorfmann, P.W:, Gupta, V., (Eds.)* Culture, Leadership, and Organizations: The GLOBE Study of 62 Societies: Thousand Oaks, CA, Sage, 2004

*Hume, D.,* A treatise of human nature. Oxford, Clarendon Press, 1978

*Hume, D.,* Enquiries concerning human understanding and concerning the principles of morals. Oxford, Clarendon Press, 1975

*Hunter, J. E., Hunter, R. F.,* Validity and utility of alternative predictors of job performance. In: Psychological Bulletin, 96, pp. 72-98, 1984

*Jung, C. G.,* Grundwerk in 9 Bänden. Walter, Düsseldorf, 1999

*Kant, I.,* Kritik der praktischen Vernunft: Hamburg, Meiner, 2003

*Kant, I.,* Was ist Aufklärung: Aufsätze zur Geschichte und Philosophie, Ed. J. Zebbe, Göttingen, 1994

*Kaplan, R. S., Norton, D. P.,* The Balanced Scorecard – Measures that Drive Performance. In: Harvard Business Review. 1992, January-February S. 71-79.

*Kaplan, R. S., Norton, D. P.,* Putting the Balanced Scorecard to work. In: Harvard Business Review. 1993, September-October S. 134-147.

*Kaplan, R. S., Norton, D. P.,* Balanced Scorecard. Strategien erfolgreich umsetzen. Stuttgart, 1997

*Kaplan, R. S., Norton, D. P.,* Strategy Maps. Der Weg von immateriellen Werten zum materiellen Erfolg. Stuttgart, 2004

*Katz, D., Macoby, N., Morse, N. C.,* Productivity, supervision and morale in an office situation. Ann Arbor, 1950

*Kauffman, S.,* At Home at the Universe. The search for the Laws of Self-Organization and Complexity. Oxford University Press, 1995

*Keirsey, David, Bates, Marilyn,* Versteh mich bitte. Charakter und Temperamenttypen. CA, USA, Prometheus Nemesis, 1990

*Kersting, Martin,* Stand, Herausforderungen und Perspektiven der Managementdiagnostik. In: Personalführung. Düsseldorf, 10/2006. DGFP (Hrsg)

*Kießling-Sonntag, Jochem,* Handbuch Mitarbeitergespräche. Berlin, Cornelsen, 2000

*Kluckhohn, F. R., Strodtbeck, F. L.,* Variations in value orientations, New York, Harper Collins, 1961

*Kohn, L. S., Diopboye, R. L.,* The effects of interview structure on recruiting outcomes. In: Journal of Applied Social Psychology, 28, pp. 821-843, 1998

*Königswieser, R.,* Widerstände gegen systemische Unternehmensführung, in: Königswieser, R., Lutz, C. (Ed.), Das systemisch evolutionäre Management. Wien, Orac, 1992

*Königswieser, Roswita, Lutz, Christian* (Ed.), Das systemisch evolutionäre Management. Wien, Orac, 1992

*Königswieser Roswita, Hillebrand Martin*, Einführung in die systemische Organisationsberatung. Heidelberg, Carl-Auer-Systeme Verlag, 2004

*Königswieser, Roswita, Exner, Alexander*, Systemische Intervention. Architekturen und Designs für Berater und Veränderungsmanager. Stuttgart, Klett-Cotta, 1998

*Kuhn, T.*, Internes Unternehmertum. München 2000

*Kutschker, M., Schmid, S.*, Internationales Management. München, Oldenbourg, 2008

*Lavan, H., Mathys, N., Drehmer, D.*, A Look at the Counseling Practices of Major U.S. Corporations, in: Personnel Administrator, 1983, Vol. 28, No. 6, 76-81, 143-146.

*Leibold, Marius, Voelpel, Sven*, Managing the Aging Workforce. Challenges and Solutions. Erlangen, Publicis, 2006

*Leibniz, G.W.*, Monadologie, Französich/Deutsch. Stuttgart, Reclam, 1998

*Levine, R.*, Eine Landkarte der Zeit. Wie Kulturen mit Zeit umgehen. München, Piper, 1997

*Levine, R., Hashimoto, T., Verma, J.*, Love and marriage in eleven cultures, in Journal of cross cultural psychology 26, 1995

*Levine, R., Conover, L.*, The Pace of Life Scale. International Society for the Study of Time, 1992

*Lewin, K.*, Field theory in social science (selected theoretical papers). New York, 1951

*Lisges,G., Schübbe, F.*, Personalcontrolling. Haufe, Freiburg 2004

*Locke, J.*, An essay concerning human understanding. Oxford, Clarendon Press, 1979

*Lord, R.G., Maher, K.J.*, Leadership and Information Processing, Linking Perceptions and Performance. People and Organizations, Vol. 1, Boston, MA, Unwin Hyman, 1991

*Lovelock, J.E.*, Healing Gaia. Harmony Books, New York, 1991

*Lueger, M.*, Macht und Herrschaft in Organisationen, in: Königswieser, R./Lutz, C. (Ed.), Das systemisch evolutionäre Management. Wien, Orac, 1992

*Luft, J. & Ingham, H.*, The Johari Window, a graphic model for interpersonal relations. Western Training Laboratory in Group Development, University of California at Los Angeles, Extension Office, 1955

*Luhmann, N.*, Einführung in die Systemtheorie. Heidelberg, Carl-Auer, 2002

*Lutz, C.*, Unternehmensführung im Zeitalter der Kommunikation, in: Königswieser, R./Lutz, C. (Ed.), Das systemisch evolutionäre Management. Wien, Orac, 1992

Porter, L.W., Lawler, E.E., Managerial Attitude and Performance. Hanenwood, Irwin, 1968

Malik, Fredmund, Führen, Leisten, Leben. München, Heyne, 2001

Margulis, L., Symbiotic Planet. New York, Basic Books, 1998

Margulis, L., Sagan, D., Microcosmos, New York, 1986

Martin, G., Sokrates. Hamburg, Rowohlt, 1967

Maslow, A., A Theory of Human Motivation. Psychological Review 50, 1943

Maturana, H.R., Varela, F.J., The Tree of Knowledge. The Biological Roots of Human Understanding. Boston, Shambhala, 1987

Maturana, H.R., Varela, F.J., Der Baum der Erkenntnis. Scherz, München, 1984

May, B., Moore, P., Lintott, C., Bang. Die ganze Geschichte des Universums. Stuttgart, Kosmos, 2007, 146

McClelland, D.C., The achieving society. NJ, Princeton, Van Nostrand, 1961

McGregor, D., The human side of Enterprise. New York, 1960

Molcho, Samy, Alles über Körpersprache. München, Goldmann, 2001

Molcho, Samy, Körpersprache im Beruf. München, Goldmann, 1988

Müller, Gabriele, Systemisches Coaching im Management. Weinheim, Beltz, 2003

Neuberger, O., Führen und geführt werden. Stuttgart, 1995

Nietzsche, F., Also sprach Zarathustra. Ditzingen, Reclam, 1986

Parsons, T., Das System moderner Gesellschaften, Weinheim, Juventa, 2003

Pelz, D.C., Influence: A key to effective leadership in the first line supervisor. in: Personnel, 29, 1952

Pestalozzi, J.H., Sämtliche Werke. Berlin, de Gruyter, 1927

Piaget, J., Meine Theorie der geistigen Entwicklung. Weinheim, Beltz, 2003

Piaget, J., Theorien und Methoden der modernen Erziehung. Frankfurt am Main, 1999

Platon, Sämtliche Dialoge, Band I und II. Hamburg, Meiner, 1988

Redfield, R., Introduction to B. Malinowski, Magic, Science and Religion. Boston: Beacon Press, 1948

Rentzsch, H.P., Erfolgreich verhandeln im weltweiten Business. Verhalten, Taktik und Strategie für internationale Meetings und Präsentationen. Wiesbaden, Gabler, 1999

Rescher, N., Warum sind wir nicht klüger? Der evolutionäre Nutzen von Dummheit und Klugheit. Stuttgart, Hirzel, 1994

Ridder, H.G., Personalwirtschaftslehre, Stuttgart, 1999

*Risse, H.,* Berkeley und der Demiurg. Requiem auf das Spiel in der Sackgasse. Vastorf, Merlin, 1983

*Schein, E. H.,* Organizational Psychologie. Englewood Cliffs, Prentice Hall, 1980

*Schein, E. H.,* Organizational Culture and Leadership. San Francisco, Jossey-Bass, 1992

*Schein, E.H.,* Organisationskultur. Bergisch Gladbach, EHP, 2003

*Scheler, Max,* Der Formalismus in der Ethik und die materiale Wertethik. Bouvier, 1954

*Scherm, M.,* Sarges, W., 360°-Feedback. Hogrefe, Göttingen 2002

*Scherm, M.,* (Ed.): 360-Grad-Beurteilungen. Hogrefe, Göttingen 2005

*Schiller, F.,* Über die ästhetische Erziehung des Menschengeschlechts (1795). Ditzingen, Reclam, 2000

*Schlippe, A. v., Schweitzer, J.,* Lehrbuch der systemischen Therapie und Beratung. Göttingen, Vandenhoeck & Ruprecht, 2007

*Scholz, Christian,* Personalmanagement. Informationsorientierte und verhaltenstheoretische Grundlagen. Vahlen, 2000

*Schulz von Thun, Friedemann,* Miteinander Reden, Band 1-3. Allgemeine Psychologie der Kommunikation. Hamburg, Rowohlt, 1981

*Sen, Amartya,* Ökonomie für den Menschen. München, dtv, 2002

*Senge, Peter,* Die fünfte Disziplin. Stuttgart, Klett-Cotta, 1998

*Simon, F.B.,* Einführung in Systemtheorie und Konstruktivismus. Heidelberg, Carl Auer, 2007

*Simons, P.R.J.,* Lernen, selbständig zu lernen – ein Rahmenmodell. In: Mandl, H., Friedrich, H.F. (Hrsg): Lern- und Denkstrategien. Analyse und Intervention. Göttingen, 1992

*Spada, Hans,* Allgemeine Psychologie. Bern, Hans Huber, 1990

*Spaemann, R.,* Sein und Gewordensein. Was erklärt die Evolutionstheorie? In: Evolutionstheorie und menschliches Selbstverständnis, Ed. R. Spaemann, P. Koslowski, R. Löw, Cicitas Resultate Band 6, Weinheim, Acta humaniora, 1984

*Sparrer, I.,* Einführung in Lösungsfokussierung und Systemische Strukturaufstellungen. Heidelberg, Carl Auer, 2007

*Sparrer, I.,* Wunder, Lösung und System. Heidelberg, Carl Auer, 2006

*Stirner, M.,* The Ego an his own. New York, Ben Tucker, 1907

*Stogdill, R.M.,* Handbook of Leadership: A survey of theory and research. New York, 1974

*Störig, H.J.,* Weltgeschichte der Philosophie. Stuttgart, Kohlhammer, 1981

*Struck, Klaus-Günter,* Der Coaching-Prozess. Der Weg zu Qualität: Leitfragen und Methoden. Erlangen, Publicis, 2006

*Tannenbaum, R., Schmidt, W.H.,* How to choose a leadership pattern. Harvard Business Review, 1958

*Taylor, F.W.,* Principles of Scientific Management, New York, Harper, 1911

*Trompenaars, F.,* Riding the Waves of Culture: Understanding Cultural Diversity in Business. Random House, 1993

*Tscheulin, D., Rausche, A.,* Beschreibung und Messung des Führungsverhaltens in der Industrie mit der deutschen Version des Ohio-Fragebogens. in: Psychologie und Praxis, 14, 1970

*Wöhe, Günter,* Einführung in die Allgemeine Betriebswirtschaftslehre. München, Vahlen, 2005

*Varela, F. J.,* Kognitionswissenschaft – Kognitionstechnik. Frankfurt am Main, Suhrkamp, 1990

*Vester, F.,* Unsere Welt – ein vernetztes System, München, dtv, 2002

*Vogelauer, W.,* Methoden-ABC im Coaching. München, Wolters-Kluwer, 2004

*von Bertalanffy, L..,* General System Theory. Foundations, Development, Applications. George Braziller, New York, 1969

*von Humboldt, W.,* Werkausgabe in 7 Bänden. Ed.Ed. Carl Brandes, ND, Berlin 1988

*Vorländer, K.,* Geschichte der Philosophie mit Quellentexten, Band 1-3. Hamburg, Rowohlt, 1990

*Weber, M.,* Soziologie. Weltgeschichtliche Analysen. Stuttgart, 1956

*Weibler, J.,* Personalführung. München, Vahlen, 2001

*Weiner, B.,* Motivationspsychologie. Weinheim, Beltz, 1994

*Weber, M.,* Wirtschaft und Gesellschaft. Tübingen, Mohr Siebeck, 1980

*Weider, P.C.,* Das 360°-Feedback in einem europäischen Versicherungsunternehmen, in: Hofmann/Köhler/Steinhoff (Ed.): Vorgesetztenbeurteilung in der Praxis. Weinheim, 1995, 159-166

*Welch, Jack & Suzy,* Winning. Frankfurt, Campus 2005

*Wiener, N.,* Cybernetics. Cambridge, MIT Press, 1948

*Wittmann, S.,* Praxisorientierte Managementethik: Gestaltungsperspektiven für die Unternehmensführung. Münster, 1994

*Zeilinger, A.,* Einsteins Spuk. Teleportation und weitere Mysterien der Quantenphysik. München, Goldmann, 2007

Nicolai Andler

# Tools for Project Management, Workshops and Consulting

**A Must-Have Compendium of Essential Tools and Techniques**

2008, 290 pages, 109 illustrations,
39 tables, hardcover
ISBN 978-3-89578-302-9, € 39.90

This best selling book is a unique reference work and guide for those wanting to learn about or who are active in the fields of consulting, project management and problem solving in general. As such, it presents cookbook-style access to more than 100 most important skills, including a rating of each tool in terms of applicability, ease of use and effectiveness.

Ulf Pillkahn

# Using Trends and Scenarios as Tools for Strategy Development

**Shaping the Future of Your Enterprise**

2008, 452 pages, 167 colored
illustrations, hardcover
ISBN 978-3-89578-304-3, € 47.90

The book presents the two most powerful tools for future planning: environmental analysis, based on the use of trends, as well as the development of visions of the future through the use of scenarios.

Marius Leibold, Sven Voelpel

# Managing the Aging Workforce

**Challenges and Solutions**

2006, 244 pages, 24 illustrations,
12 tables, hardcover
ISBN 978-3-89578-284-8, € 32.90

The aging of their workforce will have dramatic consequences. Challenges arising include leadership, health and knowledge management, diversity and innovation. This book presents an analysis of the present and upcoming situation, and concepts enterprises will need to survive.

www.publicis.de/books